VEGETARIAN SU... ...DS

Front cover: Tempeh Stir-fry (*page 44*), served with fried noddles.
Back cover: Special Chilli Con Carne (*page 47*), served in taco shells.

VEGETARIAN SUPER SOYA FOODS

Vikki Leng

THORSONS PUBLISHING GROUP
Wellingborough, Northamptonshire

First UK edition published 1988

First published 1987 by McCulloch Publishing Pty Ltd
348 Drummond Street, Carlton, Victoria 3053, Australia
in association with The Macmillan Company
of Australia Pty Ltd,
107 Moray Street, South Melbourne, Victoria, Australia

British Library Cataloguing in Publication Data

Leng, Vikki
[Super soy foods]. Vegetarian super soya
foods: an amazing variety of protein-packed
delights.
1. Cookery (Soybeans)
I. Title
641.6'5655   TX803.S6

ISBN 0-7225-1584-7

Published by Thorsons Publishers Limited,
Wellingborough, Northamptonshire, NN8 2RQ, England

Printed in Great Britain by
Richard Clay Limited, Bungay, Suffolk.

1 3 5 7 9 10 8 6 4 2

CONTENTS

INTRODUCTION

Hooray at last for an economical, easily obtained food that is not only nutritious, but can be made into an endless variety of surprisingly delicious dishes. Soya beans are available in many forms such as miso, soya-bean oil, okara, soya flour, soya grits, soya milk, soy sauce, tempeh, tofu and textured vegetable protein. You may be unfamiliar with many of these but that's where I can help — this book is bursting with quick and easy recipes that are based on soya foods.

This book is not a Bible for health fanatics but for anyone wishing to enrich their diet with valuable nutrients in the cheapest and easiest way. You need not omit fish, eggs or dairy products from your diet to enjoy the benefits of soya foods. Althought soya foods are substantially nutritious foods and can be used as alternatives to animal foods, I am not advocating this for everyone. Should you wish to introduce soya foods to your daily eating plan gradually, try adding them to familiar and favourite recipes rather than making a whole meal of them.

Behind the very humble exterior of the soya bean lies many suprising and valuable properties. Not only does the soya bean contain all the essential amino acids, thus making it a plant source of complete protein, but most soya foods also contain calcium, potassium, phosphorous and vitamins of the B complex and vitamin A. Soya sprouts are rich in vitamins C and E as an added bonus. Tempeh, being a fermented food, is also a good source of vitamin B_{12} for vegetarians.

Tofu and tempeh are two particularly popular soya foods. They have been used extensively for centuries in the East before their popularity spread to the western countries. In the USA, tofu and tempeh are popular protein sources particularly as the wholefood industry is flourishing. I'm happy to say that it seems we are following suit.

Having taught soya food cooking classes for several years, I have relished in naming the course — 'The Soya Bean-Versatility Plus!' I'd also like to say the course could have been aptly named 'The Soya Bean-Economy Plus!' Soya foods are very cheap sources of protein. Using recipes in this book, you will be able to obtain protein for a family of four for two or three meals from just 1 lb/455g soya beans.

Vegetarians have been enjoying the benefits of soya foods for years but at last the general public can learn of their nutritional value, economy, versatility and their use as a substitute for dairy and wheat products for allergy sufferers. Dairy products are an excellent source of protein, calcium, vitamin A and vitamins of the B complex for most people. However, some people suffer from an allergy to cow's milk and its products. Obviously this restricts allergy sufferers to a small range of recipes as many conventional recipes and commercially prepared foods contain cow's milk, butter or cheese. Tofu and soya milk are excellent substitutes for soft cheeses and cow's milk in any recipe. Wheat allergy sufferers are also restricted in the variety of foods they can eat; I've found soya flour and rice bran to be of great help here. I've purposefully included several 'wheatless' pie crusts, cakes and munchies in this book and I dedicate them to the anxious mothers who have telephoned me to request special recipes for their children who have a wheat allergy. I hope this book brings a little more happiness into the lives of allergy sufferers and those who cook for them!

So, you may be seeking a source of protein from plant foods, wishing to stretch your food budget further, looking for interesting and imaginative recipes to add variety to your dinner party menus or searching for meals suitable for those on a special diet.

Whatever your needs, as long as you derive even a degree of the satisfaction I have obtained from writing this book, its purpose has certainly been fulfilled.

Happy reading and even happier living!

GLOSSARY

Agar agar is a sea vegetable (Kanton) which is used as a gelatine substitute. Agar agar is used to set moulded salads, jellies, cheesecakes, sauces, jams and icecream and has the added bonus of containing protein iodine and iron. Agar agar is available:

Powdered The agar agar has been ground to a fine powder which resembles salt in colour and texture; it can be used quickly and easily. Take care that the agar agar is in pure form. Some powdered agar agars have been imported in packets and have been sweetened and flavoured. Use 1 teaspoon of powdered agar agar per 8 fl oz/240ml of liquid when preparing a jelly. You would need at least 3 teaspoons of flavoured agar agar per 8 fl oz/240ml of liquid to set a jelly. Stirring, heat the agar agar and liquid in a saucepan until simmering point is reached. Reduce heat and cook for 1 minute, stirring, to mix the agar agar evenly through the liquid.

Flakes This agar agar looks like small flakes of 'plastic'. It is fairly quick to dissolve but you must use 2-3 teaspoons per 8 fl oz/240ml of liquid when making a jelly.

Strips The agar agar has been moulded into thin strips or long rectangular blocks. It looks like aerated plastic! For quick dissolving it's best to break it into pieces and soak for ½ hour in the liquid you want to thicken. To set 8 fl oz/240ml of liquid you need a piece of agar agar about 1¼ in/3cm square and ¾ in/2cm thick.

Bean curd is another name for tofu. Many Chinese restaurant menus feature some type of bean curd dish (i.e., Bean Curd and Stir-fried Vegetables). Bean curd also features on the menus of Japanese restaurants.

Carob is obtained from the pod of a Mediterranean tree. It is a nutritious chocolate-tasting food which contains good quantities of calcium, phosphorous, iron, vitamin A and B complex vitamins. It contains a natural sugar so requires little extra sweetening. Carob is often enjoyed by 'chocaholics' because it tastes very similar to chocolate but it is a 'healthy' alternative to chocolate as it doesn't contain caffeine or oxalic acid and it is low in fat. Carob is available as:

Powder Compared to cocoa powder, carob is very sweet. It may be used in drinks, cakes, cookies, and cake icing.
Confectionery Carob is made into blocks, bars, buttons and other sweets.

Coconut cream is a delicious mixture of fresh coconut and water which has been blended until velvety smooth. Coconut cream is the consistency of thin custard and is scrumptious when used as a substitute for cream in any recipe and can also be added to blended fruit drinks, curries or dessert dishes for a touch of the exotic. Coconut cream can be obtained in cans or tetra packs from delicatessens, some supermarkets and health food shops.

Miso is paste prepared from fermented soya beans with the addition of sea salt. It is available in several colours varying from dark brownish black (Mugi Miso or Kome Miso) to a light golden colour (White Miso). Quite often other grains, such as wheat, buckwheat, barley or rice are added to the soya beans causing variation in flavour and colour; the length of time of fermentation also dictates the colour and flavour; the longer the fermentation, the darker the colour and richer the flavour. 'White Miso' is very popular as the flavour is savoury yet not overpowering. Miso contains the concentrated nutrients of soya beans with the addition of vitamin B_{12} (due to the fermentation process). It is a very easily digested food which has myriads of uses from flavouring soups, drinks and sauces to adding the 'bite' to casseroles, loaves, patties and spreads. Miso is available from health food shops and oriental grocery shops. To make an 'instant' stock, use 1-2 teaspoons of miso: 8 fl oz/240ml hot water.

Nigari is a commonly-used organic 'setting agent'. It is obtained from sea water, being the solid residue after the salt extraction process. When nigari is added to hot soya milk, curds and whey are formed and tofu can be made. Nigari is available from health food shops or oriental grocery shops. It should be stored in an airtight container to prevent the absorption of moisture from the air.

Okara is a mixture of puréed, soaked soya beans which have been cooked during the production of soya milk and tofu. It is a wonderfully versatile and nutritious food which can be made into an endless number of dishes such as burgers, loaves, pâtés, puddings, cakes, cookies and even muesli. Okara is rich in fibre and also contains protein. It may be stored in a closed container in the refrigerator for up to 1 week or frozen for several weeks. To use in crumble, toppings, muesli, burgers, loaves and bread, spread it out on a baking tray and bake at 400°F/200°C, or Gas Mark 6 for 40 minutes. This roasting process imparts a sweet, nutty flavour to the okara. It also dries it out so that it keeps for longer.

Rice bran is the outer layer of the rice grain, removed during the 'rice polishing' process. Rice bran is rich in B-vitamins and fibre and is an excellent substitute for wheat bran, wheat germ or breadcrumbs in any recipe. Rice bran has a much finer texture than wheat bran. For those allergic to wheat, rice bran can be used in pie crusts, cookies and as a substitute for bread crumbs when making burgers and loaves.

Shoyu sauce is made from a mixture of fermented soya beans and wheat and has a slightly milder flavour than tamari. Shoyu sauce is also available with a reduced salt content.

Soya beans are available fresh, dried and canned. Canned and dried soya beans are more popular due to an almost limitless shelf-life. For this reason I have based this book on the canned and dried varieties and products made from the dried beans.

Dried soya beans require pre-soaking. Thorough cooking then softens the soya beans so they can be physically broken down and digested by the body. The nutrients contained in the beans can thus be more readily absorbed.

Soya beans are an important source of protein in a vegetarian's diet as they are a plant food that contains all the essential amino acids found in meat. But remember, soya beans also contain fibre, vitamin A, B vitamins, potassium, phosphorous and calcium, so they are also valuable in the diet of the average 'meat and 2 veg' person. Soya beans not only add nutrients to your favourite recipes but will stretch your food budget further. Why not add whole soya beans to your favourite casseroles and puréed soya beans to your hamburgers and loaves?

Economically, soya beans are an amazing food. One 1 lb/455g packet of soya beans can be used to provide the main source of protein in at least two meals for four people.

Soya beans are available from delicatessens, health food shops and supermarkets. The most economical way to buy them is dried.

Dried and canned beans can be stored almost indefinitely in containers in your cupboard.

However, due to the demands upon the modern cook to produce 'instant meals', you will need to know how you can prepare the dried soya beans to make them available as last minute additions to quick meals. Canned beans are already cooked so can be used as they are.

Soya-bean oil is popular due to its mild flavour and odour. It is used for cooking as well as in salads and dressings. It is available from health food shops and supermarkets.

Soya flour is a finely textured, pale yellow flour made from soya beans. When it is added to scones, bread, cakes and cookies, it gives a sweet, nutty flavour and a golden suntan (as well as adding protein, calcium, phosphorous and potassium). Soya flour contains no gluten so should be mixed with other flours, about 1 part soya flour to 4 parts wheat flour or 1 part soya flour to 4 parts wheat and rye flour mixed.

This will allow the resulting dough to be elastic, causing the mixture to rise and ensuring an edible texture. Using all soya flour in conventional recipes will result in bread, cakes or cookies with a texture similar to a brick!

To enrich and thicken soup, blend 2-3 tablespoons of soya flour with 2 fl oz/60ml of cold water and stir into 1⅔ pints/910ml soup.

For added nutrients, flavour and thickening when making burgers and loaves, use soya flour instead of wheat flour or replace some of the breadcrumbs with soya flour.

Soya grits are roasted soya beans which have been ground to a coarse meal rather like the texture of cracked wheat. Soya grits can be used to make patties, casseroles, cakes and cookies and take less preparation and cooking time than whole soya beans. They are available at health food shops and can be valuable for the busy person who needs quickly-prepared meals.

Soya milk is a sweet, nutty milk which is made from soya beans. Its nutritional value is similar to cow's milk. Soya milk has approximately the same amount of protein and B-vitamins. It has more iron than cow's milk but less calcium. However the bonus of less fat and no cholesterol should not be overlooked.

Soya milk is often used as a cow's milk substitute for allergy sufferers. Some infants cannot tolerate cow's milk but flourish on specially prepared soya formulae which can be obtained from chemists. Children and adults can use commercially-prepared liquid soya milk which is available in tetra packs and plastic containers from health food shops. Fresh soya milk is also available in cartons. The drawback of using the liquid soya milk is the cost. Sophisticated and expensive manufacturing processes are necessary to render the soya milk suitable for most palates by modifying the 'beany' flavour and producing a smooth texture. You can make soya milk yourself (see page 20) but it does have a definite 'beany' flavour and is most suitable for use in cooking.

Soya milk is also available as powder but some brands contain lactose. This would only be a problem if the consumer was allergic to the lactose in cow's milk.

Soya milk can be used in all recipes instead of cow's milk. In some recipes it may be diluted with water to make your money stretch further.

Soy sauce is made from fermented soya beans with the addition of sea salt. It contains small amounts of protein, vitamins and minerals and some varieties contain caramel colouring.

Check the label to ensure that it is a pure product that is naturally brewed. Soy sauce is handy as an instant flavour and colour booster and is delicious for seasoning stir-fried rice and vegetables, dips, spreads and casseroles.

Soya yoghurt is made from soya milk and can be obtained from health food shops. It is quite different to yoghurt made from cow's and goat's milk, however, as it has a light curdy texture and a 'beany' flavour.

Tahini is a creamy paste made from grinding sesame seeds into a 'butter' and adding sesame or peanut oil to thin it down. It is laden with goodies such as protein and calcium and is just as versatile as it is tasty. It has a peanut-like flavour and is scrumptious added to dips and spreads, sauces, cakes, pastry, cookies and dressings.

Tamari is a pure soy sauce, like shoyu sauce except that it does not contain wheat. It is a natural food with a full-bodied, rich flavour and may be used to flavour dips, soups, casseroles and dressings. Although it contains sea salt this is preferable to pure salt. When using tamari as a seasoning you benefit from the full rich flavour of the soya beans as well as the salt.

A low-salt tamari is now available.

Tempeh is a firm cake of partially cooked soya beans held together by a mould culture. Unlike tofu, tempeh has a chewy texture and can be easily sliced or chopped and used in many recipes such as soups, casseroles, loaves, burgers, pizzas and salads. Having a more distinctive flavour than tofu, tempeh is best suited to savoury recipes.

Nutritionally, tempeh ranks high as a protein food but especially important is the vitamin B_{12} that it contains. Vitamin B_{12} is most commonly provided by animal products so is harder to obtain in the vegetarian diet. The fermentation process used to produce tempeh brings about the production of vitamin B_{12}. Like tofu, tempeh is an easily-digested food; the beans have been precooked and further tenderized by the fermentation process. Unlike tofu, however, tempeh contains fibre as it is made from the whole bean. For those used to the chewy texture and flavour of meat, tempeh is very satisfying; fried tempeh is quite similar to fried chicken or fish. Tempeh is available from oriental grocery shops and larger health food shops.

Fresh tempeh can be stored for a week to 10 days in the refrigerator. Otherwise it's best to freeze it for future use. This will not greatly affect the tempeh and after thawing can be used as for fresh tempeh. Once thawed it must be used at once. Do not freeze it for future use. Fresh tempeh should have a nutty smell. Avoid tempeh with a slimy texture and a smell of alcohol.

Tempeh can be eaten 'raw' but its flavour is developed by quick cooking methods such as stir-frying, steaming or frying and is useful as a last minute addition to quick meals.

Textured vegetable protein adds nourishment and texture to many vegetable recipes. For those who especially enjoy the chewy texture of meat, TVP makes a good substitute. Commercially prepared TVP is available from health food shops and supermarkets but you can easily make your own at home (see page 18) thereby ensuring a pure natural food, free of additives. My recipes for TVP is based on prefrozen tofu.

Once prepared and roasted, TVP can be stored in an airtight container in your cupboard for future use.

Tofu is commonly known as bean curd and is used extensively in Chinese and Japanese cooking; it is also known as soya bean cheese because it is made from soya milk. Tofu is rapidly becoming a popular Western food because of its many assets. After all, haven't we all been looking for a highly-nutritious, easily-digested, low-fat, low calorie, cholesterol-free food that is economical and versatile?

Tofu is rich in protein, vitamins (especially B vitamins) and minerals (especially calcium and iron). For those who appreciate the food value of soya beans but find them hard to digest, tofu is the answer.

Tofu contains between 33-50 % of the calories contained in the same quantity of cheese or meat and for those embarking on a low-cholesterol diet, makes a good substitute for meat, eggs and cheese. It also costs much less, yet when eaten in conjunction with cereals or vegetables is equally nutritious. Tofu is one of the most versatile foods I have ever used. It has a bland flavour, neither savoury nor sweet, so it can be used in many recipes from dips, soups and tasty casseroles to cheesecakes, desserts, cakes and ice cream.

Different types of tofu are available and some types are more suited to special recipes. *Japanese tofu* has a firm, curdy texture, the setting agent usually being nigari. Its firm texture makes it suitable for recipes such as loaves, patties and fried tofu. *Chinese* tofu has a softer texture due to the use of a different setting agent, calcium sulphate. This tofu makes creamy cheesecakes, creams and ice-cream and a scrumptious scrambled egg substitute. *Silken tofu*, as the name implies has a silky velvety texture and is very soft. It is usually available in tetra packs. Having such a delicate texture, silken tofu is best used in dessert dishes, dips or dressings, ice-cream or cakes. *Dried tofu* is also available. Its obvious asset is its long shelf-life. Dried tofu can be easily reconstituted by soaking it in hot water for 10 minutes. It can then be used very successfully in recipes which require firm tofu. An added bonus is the increased absorbency of this type of tofu. It rapidly picks up the flavour of marinades. This, together with its chewy texture, makes it an exceptionally popular food for savoury dishes.

Tofu is available at health food shops and oriental grocery shops and occasionally at supermarkets. Being a 'fresh' cheese or curd, tofu needs to be refrigerated, so you will find it in this section of the above shops. It is packaged semi-immersed in water to retain freshness. Fresh tofu is pale greyish-white in colour and has a sweet 'beany' smell. When storage is prolonged, the tofu becomes yellowish in colour, develops a 'slimy' texture and has a sour smell. It's best to find out the days the tofu is delivered to your shop so you can purchase it when it's as fresh as possible.

Storing tofu Tofu must be stored in water in a covered container in the refrigerator. If you pour the water off and replace it with fresh cold water each day, tofu can be kept for 5-7 days. Should you wish to keep tofu longer than this, you can freeze it. (See page 18.)

CHAPTER ONE

HANDY HINTS WITH SOYA FOODS

Preparing dried beans so they are ready for quick recipes

1. Soak the soya beans overnight in plenty of water. Drain them well, then store in closed containers in the refrigerator (for a week) or in the freezer (for several weeks). An added bonus of freezing the beans is that they become 'softened' and require less cooking time to make them tender.

2. For more 'instant' use, soya beans can be soaked and cooked, then cooled and stored in closed containers in your refrigerator (for one week) or in the freezer (for several weeks).

Cooking soya beans

As nutritious and versatile as soya beans are, they have proven unpopular with some people as they can cause flatulence! However, this problem can generally be relieved by pre-soaking the beans and thorough cooking. *After soaking the beans, pour the soaking water* onto your garden, then replace with fresh water for cooking. During the soaking process, enzymes responsible for adverse reactions are released from the beans. Thorough cooking is also needed to break down the tough soya bean so it can be further broken down, digested and absorbed by the body. Insufficiently cooked soya beans simply pass through the system quickly (and with discomfort) and many of the valuable elements they contain are not absorbed.

For 1½ lbs/680g cooked beans
Soak 12 oz/340g of beans overnight in 1⅔ pints/910ml of water. Drain the beans, then place in a saucepan with 1⅔ pints/910ml of water. Bring to the boil, then remove any foam that rises to the surface as this can cause boiling over. Reduce the heat and simmer until the beans are tender, at least 1 hour. Should the cooking

water evaporate, replace with more boiling water as needed. After the beans are cooked, the remaining liquid can be used as stock in other recipes. Store the liquid in the refrigerator for up to 1 week. Use the beans at once or cool them and store in the refrigerator or freezer for later use.

Sprouting soya beans

The sprouting process also renders the soya beans more digestible and gives another variation in taste and texture. The nutritional value also increases significantly. Vitamins of the B complex and vitamins C and E are synthesized during the sprouting process. Unlike most other sprouts, soya bean sprouts should be lightly steamed to make them more digestible; soya sprouts contain an enzyme which inhibits the digestion of the protein.

N.B. *Before sprouting, sort the beans, removing any broken beans as these will not sprout but will ferment and spoil the other beans.*

Soak the beans overnight in plenty of cold water. Drain them, then place in a sprouting container (such as a sprouting tube or dome) or in a glass jar with an open weave cloth spread over the open top.

Cover the beans with cool, fresh water and then drain them completely, at least three times each day. The rinsing process is necessary to cool the beans and wash away enzymes given off during the sprouting process.

Soya beans take longer to sprout than alfalfa seeds, brown lentils and mung beans — about 5-7 days. Store the soya sprouts in a covered container in the refrigerator and rinse and drain each day until they are used.

Home-made textured vegetable protein

1 lb/455g prefrozen tofu, thawed and well drained
4 tablespoons soy sauce or shoyu or tamari

Depending on the required texture, chop the tofu finely or cut into small cubes (about ¼ inch/7mm). Place in a bowl and sprinkle soy sauce over them. Mix thoroughly and allow to stand a few minutes to ensure thorough absorption of the sauce.

Spread tofu in a thin layer on a baking sheet and bake at 300°F, 150° C or Gas Mark 2 until completely dry — about 1 hour. Cool and store in an airtight container until required. To reconstitute the TVP pour 8 fl oz/240ml of boiling water or vegetable stock over each cup of TVP and allow to stand 10-15 minutes before use.

Freezing tofu

Drain all the water away from the tofu, and seal it in a freezer bag before freezing. It's important to note that the freezing process causes changes in the colour and texture of the tofu — it becomes a light brown colour and develops a 'spongy' texture. (It looks like a household sponge!) Simply thaw it and press or squeeze out any liquid. Chop the tofu finely before combining with other foods. Bonuses are that the prefrozen tofu lends a satisfying 'chewy' texture to casseroles, stews, loaves and burgers and also has a greater capacity to absorb other flavours. However, deep frying is not a recommended cooking method due to the increased absorption rate of prefrozen tofu.

An important note. Don't attempt to make dips, dressings, cheesecakes, cakes or ice-cream from prefrozen tofu. A general rule to follow is to use frozen, thawed tofu in dishes which require a 'chewy' texture similar to meat such as casseroles, burgers or meatless moussaka.

Home-made tofu

At first glance, my recipe for home-made tofu seems daunting to say the least. However, once you have made it, you will see how easy it is and you will also appreciate the fringe benefits of having a good supply of okara if you follow the directions for Tofu 1.

If you can't obtain tofu easily you can now make your own as you need it. It is also handy to be able to make your own should you need to follow kosher cooking regulations.

Economically, home-made tofu is remarkable. You can provide a family of four with protein food from 12 oz/340g of soya beans for two meals. Prepare 1 lb/455g of tofu as the recipe states and use it for any of the tofu recipes for one meal. For the second meal, use the okara for patties, a loaf or a casserole.

To press and drain the tofu you will need a tofu press or a colander. Tofu presses are available from some health food shops. They are stainless steel or wooden boxes with drainage holes. They have a slightly smaller 'pressing plate' which is placed on top of the tofu and weighted down to press the whey out.

Tofu 1 — using soya beans

This seems the most complicated and is the most time-consuming method of making tofu, but is the most economical.

Equipment:
Large saucepan, about gallon/4.5l capacity
Long-handled wooden spoon
Sieve
Tofu press (or colander and dessert plate)
Large bowl to contain the hot soya milk
Cheesecloth or muslin, about 14 inches/36cm square

Food processor or blender
Rubber gloves!
Container for storing tofu

Ingredients: For about 1 lb/455g of tofu
12 oz/340 soya beans washed
Water
2 teaspoons nigari dissolved in 4 tablespoons of water

Soak the beans in 3⅔ pints/2.13l of water for 12-16 hours. (In warm weather, keep the beans soaking in the refrigerator to prevent fermentation.) Blend the beans and water until foamy, about 60 seconds.

Place the mixture in the large saucepan and add a further 4 pints/2.27l water. Bring to the boil, stirring occasionally with the wooden spoon to prevent sticking to the bottom of the saucepan. Watch that the mixture does not boil over. Reduce the heat to a gentle simmer and cook for 15 minutes.

Place the sieve over the large bowl, then line it with the cheeselcoth. Put on the rubber gloves to prevent burnt hands during the next step. Pour the hot mixture into the sieve and strain it through the cheesecloth by pulling up the edges and twisting them together firmly. The liquid in the bowl is **soya milk** and can be cooled and stored in the refrigerator for use as a cow's milk substitute, or continue with the recipe for tofu.

The pulpy mixture in the cheesecloth is **okara**. Cool the okara and store it in a covered container in the refrigerator.

Pour the soya milk back into the saucepan and heat to just below boiling point (192°F/80°C). Stir the milk briskly in a circular fashion and pour in the nigari. Allow the mixture to stand for 5 minutes to allow the curds and whey to form. (If this does not happen, dissolve an additional ½ teaspoon nigari in 1 tablespoon of water and stir into the soya milk.)

Line the colander or tofu press with the clean cheesecloth and stand it over the large bowl to collect the whey. Pour the mixture into the tofu press (or colander) carefully and fold the edges of the cloth over the top of the tofu. Put the pressing plate on top and place 2 lb/900g weight on top of that. (I usually use a jar of beans.)

Allow the tofu to stand for 1 hour, then unwrap it and place it in a container. Carefully cover it with cold water and store in the refrigerator.

Tofu 2 — using soya milk

Try preparing tofu from soya milk. The most economical soya milk apart from making your own from soya beans is the reconstituted soya milk powder. Though you will not obtain okara as a by-product, this method is quick and easy and the resulting tofu is quite similar to my first recipe.

Equipment:
Large saucepan
Wooden spoon
Tofu press (or colander and dessert plate)
Cheesecloth
Container for storing tofu

Ingredients: For 1 lb/455g of tofu
3½ pints/2l of soya milk
2 teaspoons nigari dissolved in 4 tablespoons of water

Stirring occasionally, heat the soya milk to just below boiling point (about 190°F/80°C). Stir the milk briskly in a circular fashion and pour in the nigari. Cover and allow to stand for 5 minutes to allow the curds and whey to form.

Line the tofu press (or colander) with cheesecloth. Pour the curds and whey into the cheesecloth. Fold the edges over the curds and place the pressing place on top of the cloth.

Place a 2 lb/900g weight (such as a jar of beans) on top of the plate and allow to stand for 1 hour.

Unwrap the tofu and carefully place in a container. Carefully cover the tofu with water and store in the refrigerator for future use.

Tofu 3 — using soya flour

You can also use soya flour to make tofu. This method is also quick and easy, but again, you will not obtain okara as a by-product. This tofu also has more of a granular texture and is darker in colour than Tofu 1 or 2 and so I suggest this tofu be used for burgers and loaves rather than for dishes which require a smooth texture.

Equipment:
Large saucepan
Wooden spoon
Fine sieve
Tofu press (or colander and dessert plate)
Cheesecloth
Container for storing tofu

Ingredients: For 1 lb/455g of tofu
8 oz/225g soya flour
3½ pints/2l water
2 teaspoons nigari dissolved in 4 tablespoons water

Blend the soya flour to a smooth paste with some of the water then mix in the remaining water. Place in a large saucepan and bring to the boil, stirring occasionally to prevent sticking. Simmer for 5 minutes. Strain the hot mixture through a fine sieve. Stir the milk briskly in a circular fashion, then pour in the nigari. Cover and stand for 5 minutes to allow the curds and whey to form.

Line the colander or tofu press with the cheesecloth and pour the curds in. Fold the edges of the cheesecloth over the tofu then cover with the pressing plate. Top with a 2 lb/900g weight (such as a jar of beans) and allow to stand for I hour.

Unwrap the tofu and carefully place in a container. Carefully cover with water and store in the refrigerator for future use.

Other hints

Soya foods can be used to enrich your favourite recipes. Here are a few suggestions.

Cheesecakes

Tofu can be used instead of, or together with cream, ricotta or cottage cheeses.

Dips

You can replace cottage, ricotta or cream cheese with tofu in any recipe. Remember when replacing soft cheeses, *silken* tofu is the best type to use.

Ice-cream

Soya milk can be used instead of, or together with cow's milk. Tofu can be blended with the ingredients also. Add about 9 oz/255g tofu to each 1¾ pints/litre of milk used, soya milk powder can be added to the tofu ice-cream also. For a smooth ice-cream, the tofu should be mixed with a hot liquid such as soya milk or fruit juice so that it becomes lightly cooked. Cooked tofu can be frozen and still retains its smooth texture. Frozen raw tofu can become stringy or granular even after it has been blended.

Milk shakes

Soya milk can be used instead of or together with cow's milk. Soya milk powder can be added to give an especially 'fluffy' milkshake. Use 2-3 teaspoons soya milk powder for each cup of milk used.

Lasagne

Use ¼ inch/½cm slices of tofu instead of the layer of cheese sauce. For added flavour, first sprinkle the tofu with a little soy sauce. Alternatively, mashed tofu can be added to the Bolognese sauce in your recipe. If using cheese sauce, soya milk can be used to make this also.

Pastry, pancakes, bread, cakes, biscuits and muffins

Replace up to ¼ of the wheat flour in the recipe with soya flour. For cakes, pancakes and muffins, add 2 teaspoons of baking powder to every cup of soya flour. Adding soya flour not only adds nutrients to the recipes but also gives a richer, golden colour and a nutty flavour. Bakery items containing soya flour also have a softer crumb and a moist texture due to the moisture retaining property of soya flour. Moist, cholesterol-free baked goods can be prepared by using tofu and oil instead of butter. For each 4 oz/125g butter needed, use 3½ oz/100g tofu and 3 tablespoons of oil. Using an electric beater or food processor to cream the tofu and oil together first will ensure thorough mixing as well as incorporating air into the mixture.

Patties

Vegetable patties can be made by mixing equal quantities of well drained mashed tofu or tempeh with vegetables. Mash the ingredients well and add chopped or minced onion and parsley to taste. Season with a little salt and freshly-ground pepper to taste and mix in enough soya flour to thicken the mixture before forming into patties. The patties can be coated with a little soya flour before frying them until golden brown in a little oil.
Note: Adding tofu or tempeh and soya flour to the patty mixture means that they will bind together without the addition of a beaten egg. However, egg may still be added if you wish.

Quiches and flans

Add tofu to your eggs when beating them to make filling for quiches and flans. Use 4¼ oz/125g tofu, 3 eggs and 8-12 fl oz/240-340ml milk to fill a 9½ inch/24cm pastry case. Don't forget to add plenty of flavour to your filling. Chopped or minced onion and fresh herbs with a dash of soy sauce are especially tasty additions.

Soups

Blend 2-3 tablespoons soya flour with 6 tablespoons of water until it forms a smooth paste. Add to your favourite soup to thicken and flavour it. The above quantity of soya flour will thicken 1⅔-2 pints/1.17l of soup or stock from stew.
    Why not add cooked soya beans to soups and stews as well. This adds a texture contrast as well as nutrients.

Souper Tempeh Try adding a boost in nutrition, flavour and texture to your favourite soups by adding tempeh. Cut the tempeh into small cubes or strips and add to the hot soup, cooking gently for 10 minutes before serving. For a sweet, nutty flavour, first fry the small pieces of tempeh until golden brown in a little oil. Crispy fried tempeh is also delicious sprinkled on top of soups before serving.

Stuffed vegetables

Use equal quantities of mashed tofu, tempeh or textured vegetable protein and minced meat or poultry for the stuffing. Okara or cooked, puréed soya beans can also be mixed into the mixture for a firmer texture.

White sauce

Use soya milk instead of or as well as cow's milk. Follow your basic white sauce recipe and method as usual.

CHAPTER TWO

SOUPS, STARTERS AND SNACKS

MISO SOUPER MAGIC

The basis for a good 'full bodied' soup is the stock. However, stockmaking is usually a time consuming procedure and time, unfortunately, is something most of us seem short of when it comes to preparing daily meals. Miso has been the answer for me when making delicious soups quickly. As you will see by the following recipes, miso is added just before serving and a nutritious, tasty soup can be whipped up in a matter of 20 minutes.

MISO SOUP

1²/₃ pints/910ml boiling water or soup
2 tablespoons white miso or 1 tablespoon dark miso

Blend the miso with 2-4 fl oz/60-115ml of the hot water (or soup) then mix with the remaining liquid. Be sure to add the miso just before serving for maximum nutritional value. Adding the miso at the beginning of the cooking time causes nutrient loss.

Note: For a sweet nutty flavour and for soups with a pale or rich orange or red colour (e.g., pumpkin) use white miso or soba miso. For soups requiring a more definite flavour and colour, use one of the dark, strong flavoured misos, such as mugi or kome miso.

As a general rule, I use white miso as a substitute for chicken stock and one of the darker misos when beef stock is called for.

CLEAR MISO SOUP

Cooking time — 25-30 minutes   *Serves 6*

½ turnip, scrubbed and diced
I carrot, scrubbed and diced
I stick celergy, washed and chopped
½ medium size swede, peeled and diced
I onion, chopped
I potato, scrubbed and diced
2-2½ pints/I-1.4l water
I½ tablespoons white miso or I tablespoon dark miso
Freshly ground black pepper to taste
A little freshly chopped parsley

Place the vegetables and the water in a large saucepan and bring to the boil. Reduce the heat to a simmer and cook until the vegetables are tender — about 25 minutes.

Blend the miso with a little of the soup and mix thoroughly with the rest of the soup. Stir in the parsley and freshly ground black pepper to taste and serve piping hot.

This soup is even more delicious reheated the next day.

VARIATIONS

Try adding 12 oz/340g cooked soya beans to make a 'meal in a bowl'. For a thicker soup blend 2½-3 tablespoons soya flour with a little water and stir into the soup before adding the miso. Stirring, bring the soup to the boil, then reduce the heat and simmer while stirring for I minute.

MISO AND MUSHROOM SOUP

Cooking time — 15-20 minutes   *Serves 6*

I-2 tablespoons oil
I onion, chopped
I potato, scrubbed and chopped
I lb/500g mushrooms, washed and chopped
I clove garlic, crushed
A little salt to taste
Pinch of sweet basil
2½ pints/I.4l water
I tablespoon dark miso or 2 tablespoons white miso and
I tablespoon soy sauce

Heat the oil gently and cook the onion and potato over a moderate heat, stirring for 2 minutes. Add the mushrooms, garlic and sweet basil and stir well. Add the water and bring to the boil.

Reduce the heat to a simmer and cook for about 10-15 minutes so that the potato cooks thoroughly. Blend until smooth with the miso then season to taste with the salt. Reheat gently and serve piping hot.

SPICY PUMPKIN AND TOFU SOUP
Cooking time — 25 minutes   Serves 4

A colourful and tasty start to a winter meal or a meal in itself when sprinkled with roasted nuts, pepitas or grated tasty cheese and accompanied by wholemeal bread and a crispy side salad

1 tablespoon oil
1 large onion, chopped
2 teaspoons ground cumin
2 teaspoons ground coriander
1¾ lb/750g pumpkin, chopped
2 pints/1.1l water
2 tablespoons white or soba miso
9 oz/250g tofu, cut in ¾ inch/2cm pieces
Salt to taste
Pepitas (pumpkin kernels), roasted nuts or
grated tasty cheese

Heat the oil gently with the onion, cumin and coriander, stirring for 1 minute. Stir in the chopped pumpkin and cook over low to moderate heat for another 2 minutes. Add the water and bring to the boil. Reduce the heat and simmer gently until the pumpkin is tender, about 20 minutes.

Stir in the miso and salt to taste, then allow to cool for 15 minutes or so. Blend until smooth with the tofu. Reheat gently to prevent curdling. Serve at once with the pepitas (or nuts or grated cheese).
Note: For a boost in the spicy flavour, add 3 teaspoons curry powder to the spices.

GOLDEN TEMPEH SOUP

Cooking time — 25 minutes   Serves 6

2 tablespoons oil
4 oz/125g tempeh, cut into small cubes or strips
1 onion, chopped
1 medium carrot, washed and cut into small
cubes
1 stick celery, washed and cut into small cubes
½ turnip, washed and cut into small cubes
Small handful of parsley, washed and chopped
1 tablespoon white miso
Water to cover (about 1⅔ pints/910ml)
A little salt and freshly ground black pepper
to taste

Heat the oil in a saucepan and fry the tempeh until golden brown. Drain on kitchen towels.

Add the chopped onion, carrot, celery and turnip and cook, stirring over moderate heat for a few minutes.

Cover with water and bring to the boil. Reduce the heat and simmer gently for about 15 minutes. Blend the miso with a little of the hot liquid, then stir it through the soup with the parsley and the tempeh.

Season to taste with the salt and pepper and serve piping hot.

TEMPEH AND LEEK SOUP

Cooking time — 30 minutes   Serves 6

1 small onion, chopped
1 tablespoon oil
1 small bunch leeks
1 silverbeet leaf, washed and finely shredded
Water to cover (about 1⅔ pints/910ml)
1 tablespoon white miso
A little salt and freshly ground pepper to
taste
3½-4 oz/100-125g tempeh, cut into small cubes or strips

Heat the oil gently and fry the onion for a few minutes. Wash the leeks thoroughly and trim coarse ends off. Cut in thin slices and place in a sieve. Rinse under running water to wash away any remaining soil. Shake dry and add to the onion. Stir over moderate heat, cooking for 5 minutes.

Cover with water and bring to the boil. Reduce the heat and cook gently for 10 minutes. Blend the miso in a little of the hot soup and then add to the saucepan with the shredded silverbeet and the tempeh. Cook gently for 10 minutes. Season with salt and pepper and serve piping hot.

CLEAR TOFU SOUP

Cooking time — 15 minutes   Serves 4

A light and nourishing soup which is quick, easy and low in calories

9 oz/250g tofu, cut into ½ inch/1cm cubes
2 tablespoons soy sauce, tamari or shoyu sauce
2 pints/1.1l water or vegetable stock
1 tablespoon dark miso or 2 tablespoons white miso
1 onion finely chopped
1 stick celery, chopped
4 spring onions, chopped
Small handful of parsley, chopped
4 oz/115g shredded spinach, cabbage or silverbeet
A little salt and freshly ground black pepper

Sprinkle the tofu with the soy sauce (or tamari or shoyu sauce) and allow to marinate for 15 minutes. Meanwhile place all the other ingredients, except the shredded spinach (or cabbage or silverbeet), in a medium saucepan and bring to the boil. Simmer gently until the vegetables are tender, about 10-15 minutes.

Carefully stir in the shredded greens and the tofu and simmer gently for 2 minutes.

Season to taste with the salt and black pepper and serve at once.

AMAZING AVOCADO DIP

Serves 4

What a delicious way to make one avocado stretch. Quite often avocadoes are on the 'forbidden food' list when it comes to low-fat and low-calorie diets. By combining avocadoes with tofu (low fat, low in calories) you can produce a dish moderate in fat and calories

9 oz/250g tofu, drained
2 cloves garlic, crushed
Juice of 1 lemon
½ white onion
1 small-medium sized ripe avocado
Small handful of fresh parsley
A little salt to taste
1-2 tablespoons tahini (optional)

Blend together until creamy. Serve with corn chips, vegetable sticks and/or pitta bread. Also delicious as a sandwich spread.

VARIATIONS

Try adding a pinch of chilli powder and 1 ripe tomato before blending. This is similar to guacamole dip. For a thinner consistency, blend in 4 fl oz/115ml yoghurt.

SOYA PÂTÉ

Cooking time — 20 minutes   Serves 4-6

Full of flavour and food value, this quickly-prepared pâté is great with crackers or pumpernickel bread or used as a sandwich spread
Note: Even though this recipe is based on okara, cooked puréed soya beans make an excellent substitute

1 tablespoon oil
1 onion, chopped
2 cloves garlic, crushed (optional)
¾ lb/340g okara or cooked, puréed soya beans
8 fl oz/240ml vegetable stock
2 tablespoons tamari or shoyu sauce
3 tablespoons tahini or peanut butter
2 teaspoons miso mixed with 8 fl oz/240ml water

Freshly ground black pepper (optional)
3 tablespoons freshly chopped parsley

Heat the oil in a frying pan and cook the onion and garlic gently for 2 minutes, stirring. Add the okara (or beans) and stir over a moderate heat for 3-4 minutes. Add the stock and bring to the boil. Reduce the heat and cook gently for 15 minutes, stirring occasionally. Remove from the heat and using a food processor, blend in tamari (or shoyu sauce), tahini (or peanut butter), pepper and parsley.

Serve in a bowl with crackers, pumpernickel or a combination of raw and steamed vegetables.

You can store this pâté in an airtight container in the refrigerator for 1 week.

PÂTÉ VARIATIONS

Omit the vegetable stock and stir in 5 oz/140g of chopped mushrooms and 4 tablespoons of water instead.

Surprisingly scrumptious. Stir in 3 tablespoons sesame seeds when cooking the onion and garlic. Cook them until they become golden brown before adding the remaining ingredients.

Stir in ½-¾ teaspoon chilli powder when cooking the onion and garlic. Omit the vegetable stock and stir in 4 ripe chopped tomatoes instead.

Stir in 2-3 teaspoons curry powder when cooking the onion and garlic.

TOFU HUMMUS

Serves 6

An instant dip which is terrifically tasty and very versatile, tofu hummus also makes a great sandwich spread

13 oz/375g tofu
3 tablespoons tahini
2 tablespoons soy sauce
3 cloves garlic, crushed
3 spring onions or ½ white onion
Juice of 1 lemon
Freshly ground black pepper

Blend all the ingredients well until smooth. Serve at once or store in a closed container in the refrigerator for 3-4 days.

TERRIFIC TOFU DRESSING

Add 4-8 fl oz/115-240ml of natural yoghurt or soya milk to the above ingredients before blending. Serve as an accompaniment to hot vegetables or crispy salads.

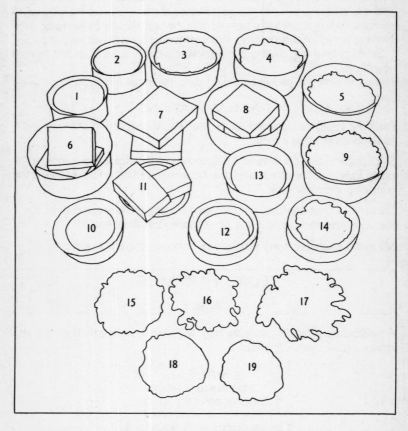

A group of soya food products which show the versatility of the soya bean. They are:
1. White miso (shiro) 2. Dark miso (mugi) 3. Soya yoghurt 4. TVP chunks 5. TVP mince
6. Prefrozen tofu 7. Dried tofu 8. Fresh tofu 9. Okara 10. Soya-bean oil 11. Tempeh
12. Soy sauce (tamari) 13. Soya milk 14. Nigari 15. Soya grits 16. Dried soya beans 17. Soyeroni
(not yet available) 18. Soya crunch (not yet available in the UK) 19. Soya flour.

BAKED MUSHROOM SOUFFLÉ

Cooking time — 15-20 minutes, ramekins
30-35 minutes, casserole   Serves 4

For best effect, bake in individual ramekins. If you like, you can sprinkle the soufflé with a little grated tasty cheese, sesame seeds, chopped nuts or breadcrumbs before baking. Serve with a leafy salad or sprouts and wholemeal rolls

2 tablespoons oil
1 onion, chopped
9 oz/250g mushrooms, washed, trimmed and chopped
Pinch of sweet basil
2 tablespoons tahini
A little salt and black pepper
1 lb/500g tofu, cut into pieces or 9 oz/250g tofu and 2
eggs
8 fl oz/240ml soya milk or yoghurt
Freshly chopped parsley
Tomato slices for decoration and fresh sweet
basil

Brush 4 individual soufflé dishes or ramekins with a little oil. Heat the oil in a frying pan with the onion and cook, stirring over moderate heat for 1-2 minutes. Add the mushrooms and parsley and continue cooking and stirring for 3 minutes. Season to taste with the sweet basil and salt and pepper.

Blend the tofu (or tofu and eggs) until smooth with soya milk (or yoghurt) and tahini, then blend in the mushroom mixture. Pour into individual ramekins and bake at 400°F, 200°C or Gas Mark 6 until golden. Decorate with the tomato slices and sweet basil leaves and serve.

Previous page, left: Spicy Pumpkin and Tofu Soup (page 27) (background) and Clear Miso Soup (page 26) are just two of the delicious soups based on miso stock
Previous page, right: Avocado and Tofu Mousse (page 36)
Left: Colourful Tempeh Stir-Fry (page 44) (background) and Tofu and Spinach Quiche (page 59) make excellent main-course dishes

TOFU TOMATOES

Cooking time — 20 minutes   Serves 6

A delicious and colourful entrée or light meal when served with a salad or baked vegetables

6 medium-large tomatoes
13 oz/375g tofu, drained and mashed
1 tablespoon oil
A few chopped spring onions or ½ onion,
chopped
½ teaspoon turmeric powder
A little salt
A little freshly chopped parsley
1¾ oz/20g breadcrumbs
1 tablespoon sesame seeds

Cut the tops off the tomatoes, then scoop out the flesh and seeds, using a teaspoon (save to use in juices, soups, casseroles or sauces). Heat the oil in a small saucepan and add the onion and turmeric powder. Cook over low-moderate heat for 1-2 minutes. Add the tofu and cook, stirring, for 3-4 minutes. Remove from the heat, then stir in the salt and parsley.

Place tomatoes on a baking sheet, then fill each one with tofu mixture. Mix breadcrumbs and sesame seeds, then sprinkle on top of tomatoes. Bake at 400°F, 200°C or Gas Mark 6 for 10-15 minutes. Serve hot or cold.

VARIATIONS

Use 9 oz/250g mashed tofu and stir in 6 oz/170g steamed peas or other cooked vegetables before filling the tomatoes.

Top each tomato with a slice of tasty cheese instead of the breadcrumbs and sesame seeds before baking.

CASHEW CROQUETTES

Cooking time — White Sauce, 5 minutes
Frying Croquettes, 5 minutes   Makes about 8

5 oz/140g cashews
4 slices wholemeal bread
1 onion, peeled and coarsely chopped
4 or 5 sprigs parsley
8 fl oz/240ml thick White sauce (see page 88)
Soya flour
4 fl oz/115ml soya milk or 1 egg beaten
½ lb/225g soya crunch
Oil for frying

Put the cashews in a food processor with the chopping blade and process to a meal. Add the bread, onion and parsley and process until all ingredients are finely chopped.

Tip mixture into a bowl and mix in the thick White sauce. Form into croquettes and roll in soya flour. Dip in soya milk (or beaten egg) and roll in soya crunch. If possible, stand for 5 or 10 minutes as this will allow the croquettes to become firm and the coating to 'set'.

Heat the oil and fry the croquettes until golden brown. Drain on absorbent paper and serve at once.

VARIATION

Rather than frying them you can bake the croquettes instead. Brush a baking sheet with a little oil and arrange the croquettes so there is some space in between.

Bake at 425°F, 220°C or Gas Mark 7 until golden brown — about 12-15 minutes.

AVOCADO AND TOFU MOUSSE

Serves 6

This is a delightful start to a meal as an entrée, served in a crisp lettuce cup with tomato wedges. It also complements a salad main meal and is delicious served with crusty wholemeal rolls
Note: *For a pale green coloured mousse, use the soya milk. For a 'bitey' flavour, use the tomato juice*

15 fl oz/425ml tomato juice or soya milk
2 teaspoons agar agar powder
1 large ripe avocado, peeled and stone removed
1 white onion, chopped
Freshly ground black pepper
A little salt to taste
9 oz/250g tofu
2 cloves garlic, crushed (optional)
Pinch of chilli powder
Handful of fresh parsley
Sliced avocado and pepper and black
olives to decorate

Place the tomato juice (or soya milk) in a saucepan and sprinkle the agar agar powder on top. Bring to the boil, stirring, then reduce the heat and stir at simmering point for 1 minute.

Cool until the mixture stops steaming but is still warm.

Blend the avocado, onion, black pepper, salt, tofu, garlic and chilli powder until smooth. While the blender or processor is in operation, add the warm agar agar mixture and blend all the ingredients well. Pour into a wetted mould or individual moulds and allow to set.

Chill in refrigerator for an hour. Serve on a bed of chopped spinach decorated with avocado slices, strips of red pepper and a few black olives.

SPROUTED SOYA PANCAKES

Cooking time — 5 minutes   Makes about 12

Packed with protein, these scrumptious pancakes make an interesting starter or a great accompaniment for hot soup or salad

4 oz/115g wholemeal self-raising flour
2 oz/55g soya flour
1 teaspoon baking powder
1 egg or 1 tablespoon arrowroot
8 fl oz/240ml soya milk
2 oz/55g sprouts — alfalfa, lentil or bean
2 spring onions, finely chopped
Salt and freshly ground pepper or 1 tablespoon soy
sauce
2 tablespoons oil, butter or margarine for frying

Blend the flour, baking powder, egg (or arrowroot) and soya milk until smooth and creamy — about 30-60 seconds. Stir in the sprouts, spring onions and salt and pepper (or soy sauce). Allow to stand for 10 minutes to allow the mixture to thicken.

Heat the oil (or butter or margarine) and fry large spoonfuls of the mixture until golden brown each side. Serve piping hot.

VARIATIONS

Try adding chopped parsley, finely chopped celery, grated carrot or sweet corn instead of bean sprouts.

TOASTY CHEESY SURPRISE

Cooking time — 3-4 minutes   Serves 4

A tasty, toasty meal in a minute. An especially good lunch or breakfast treat

9 oz/250g tofu, drained
4 teaspoons tamari or shoyu sauce
4 slices of wholemeal or pumpernickel bread
A little butter, margarine or tahini paste
4 slices tasty cheese
A little sweet paprika
4 thick slices of ripe tomato
Alfalfa sprouts or freshly chopped parsley

Cut the tofu into 4 slices and arrange them on a plate. Sprinkle each with 1 teaspoon tamari (or shoyu sauce). Toast the bread until golden brown on one side, then spread the untoasted side with butter (or margarine or tahini paste). Top each piece of toast with a slice of tofu, then a slice of cheese.

Grill until the cheese bubbles then sprinkle with a little sweet paprika. Top with a slice of tomato and a clump of alfalfa sprouts (or parsley).

DELICIOUS SANDWICH FILLINGS

Mix together the following combinations, then use as a filling for wholemeal bread, muffins or pitta bread. All the fillings are tasty with alfalfa or bean sprouts, cress or chopped or shredded lettuce . . .

1. 9 oz/250g tofu, drained and mashed, 2 tablespoons toasted sesame seeds, 1-2 tablespoons tahini paste, 1 tablespoon white miso, 1 stick celery, finely chopped, a little freshly ground black pepper.
2. 9 oz/250g tofu, drained, mashed, 2 tablespoons toasted sunflower seeds, 4 spring onions chopped, 1-1½ tablespoons tamari or shoyu sauce, 4-6 mushrooms, chopped.
3. 9 oz/250f tofu, drained, mashed, 4 spring onions, finely chopped, ¼ red pepper, finely chopped, 1 tablespoon tamari or shoyu sauce.
4. 9 oz/250g tofu, drained, mashed, 3 oz/85g raisins, chopped, 2 tablespoons toasted sunflower seeds or chopped almonds, ½ apple, finely diced, small squeeze of lemon juice.
5. 9 oz/250g tofu, drained, mashed, 3 oz/85g dried apricots, chopped, 4 or 5 dates, chopped, 1-2 teaspoons honey, ¼ teaspoon ground cinnamon.

GERRY'S CHEESELESS CHEESE

Cooking time — 40 minutes   For 1 small loaf tin

During a 'Soya bean Class' one of my students requested a recipe for a cheese substitute. Cheeseless cheese looks and tastes similar to tasty cheese but the texture is more like that of a terrine and it makes a great sandwich filling as well

1 lb/500g tofu, drained
1 level teaspoon turmeric
1 teaspoon salt
2½ oz/70g roasted sesame seeds
1 level teaspoon mustard
3 tablespoons tahini
3 tablespoons soya-bean oil or other 'low flavoured' oil
1 onion, chopped
2 oz/55g soya flour or soya milk powder

Blend all the ingredients together thoroughly and place in a lightly oiled loaf tin. Make the top smooth and sprinkle with a little water or soya milk. Bake at 350°F, 180°C or Gas Mark 4 until firm and golden brown. Serve hot or cold in slices with crusty wholemeal bread, fresh greens, tomato slices and olives.

SUPER SOYA SHAKE

Serves 2

A delicious, nutritious and refreshing drink which makes a quick 'instant' breakfast with a handful of nuts

¾ pint/425ml icy cold soya milk
A little ice
2 teaspoons honey
2 bananas or 2 oz/55g washed strawberries or
4 teaspoons carob powder
1 tablespoon soya milk powder

Blend all together well until velvety smooth. Drink at once.

PEANUTLESS PEANUT BUTTER

8 fl oz/240ml tahini
2 tablespoons white miso

Mix the two ingredients well in a cup and store in the fridge. Try using it instead of butter or margarine when making salad rolls or sandwiches.

CHAPTER THREE

MAIN MEALS

SCRUMPTIOUS SCRAMBLED TOFU

Cooking time — 6-7 minutes   Serves 4

2-3 teaspoons oil
4 spring onions, chopped or ½ onion,
chopped
½ teaspoon turmeric
1 lb/500g tofu, drained and mashed
A little salt to taste
A little freshly ground black pepper

Heat oil gently in a small-medium saucepan with the onions and turmeric powder. Stir over low-moderate heat for 1 minute. Stir in the mashed tofu, salt and pepper and continue to stir over moderate heat for 5-6 minutes. Serve hot with wholemeal toast and grilled tomatoes or use cold as a sandwich filling. It is especially good used as a filling for toasted sandwiches.

VARIATIONS

Try adding 3 oz/85g grated vegetables (e.g., carrot, pumpkin) or 3 oz/85g finely chopped vegetables (e.g., celery, pepper) at the same time as the spring onions.

Try adding 1-2 tablespoons chopped herbs (e.g., parsley, coriander) at the same time as the tofu.

FRIED TOFU

Marinading time — 15 minutes
Cooking time — 5-10 minutes   Serves 4-6

Fried tofu is versatile and is delicious added to stir-fried vegetables or rice served with a tasty sauce and steamed vegetables. Cubes of fried tofu also make a great filling for pitta bread sandwiches. Try adding a well-flavoured dip and some alfalfa or mung bean sprouts

1 lb/500g tofu, drained well
4 tablespoons tamari or shoyu sauce
Soya flour or wholemeal flour for coating
tofu
Oil for frying

Cut the tofu into ¾ inch/2cm cubes or ½ inch/1cm slices and arrange on a plate. Sprinkle tamari (or shoyu sauce) over them and allow to marinade for at least 15 minutes. (This can be done in the morning, then the slices refrigerated until you want to cook them later in the day.)

Drain off the excess tamari (or shoyu sauce, and keep in the refrigerator for flavouring sauces, soups, etc.) Roll the tofu in the flour. Heat ½ inch/1cm depth of oil in a frying pan or wok, then fry the slices of tofu until golden brown all over. Drain well on absorbent paper and serve hot or cold.

CRUMBED TOFU

After marinading and before frying, dip the flour-coated tofu slices in beaten egg. Roll in breadcrumbs and then fry as above. If possible, once the tofu slices have been coated with breadcrumbs let them stand in the refrigerator for 30 minutes or so. This will give the crumbs a chance to 'set' on the tofu slices. In fact, crumbed tofu can be prepared this way and stored in the refrigerator for a day or two before frying.

GRILLED TOFU

Use ¼ inch/5mm thick slices of tofu. Marinade in soy sauce or tamari as above. Using a moderate-high heat, grill the tofu for 5 minutes each side. For a bubbly, brown surface, first brush with a little oil or tahini using a pastry brush.

GRILLED SESAME TOFU

Sprinkle ¼ inch/5mm thick slices of tofu with sesame seeds after brushing with oil or tahini. Take care not to burn the seeds while grilling. Cook under moderate, rather than high heat.

CRISPY CRUSTY TOFU

Marinading time — 30 minutes
Cooking time — 15-20 minutes   Serves 4

Light and tasty, this is a nourishing entrée or light meal. Serve with sprouts or a leafy salad

1 lb/500g tofu, drained
1 tablespoon oil or tahini paste
4 tablespoons tamari or shoyu sauce
⅔ pint/340ml tomato or pineapple juice
1-2 cloves garlic, crushed
Freshly ground black pepper
6 oz/170g wheatgerm or breadcrumbs

Cut the tofu into ¾ inch/2cm cubes and place in a bowl with the oil (or tahini), tamari (or shoyu sauce), juice, garlic and pepper. Allow to stand for at least 30 minutes to marinade. The tofu will absorb the flavours of the other ingredients. Brush a baking sheet with a little oil.

Drain the tofu (keep the liquid to add to soups or sauces), then roll in wheatgerm (or breadcrumbs). Place the tofu on the baking sheet, then bake at 400°F, 200°C or Gas Mark 6 until golden brown — about 15-20 minutes.

VARIATION

Add 1 tablespoon grated root ginger to the oil, tamari, juice, garlic and pepper mixture before marinading.

TEMPEH STIR-FRY

Cooking time — 12-15 minutes *Serves 4*

13 oz/375g tempeh
Oil for frying, about 4 tablespoons
½ bunch spring onions
I medium carrot, scrubbed and cut into strips
I stick celery, cut into strips or I medium
courgette, cut into strips
½ medium pepper, cut into strips
Handful of green beans, topped, tailed and
cut in half
I medium tomato, cut in wedges or 2½ oz/75g
sliced mushrooms
2 tablespoons soy sauce

Cut the tempeh into strips. Heat the oil and cook the tempeh over a moderate heat until golden brown and crunchy. Remove from the oil and drain well on kitchen towels. Retain I tablespoon oil in pan or wok and fry the spring onions, carrot, celery (or courgette), pepper and beans, stirring for 5 minutes over moderate heat.

Stir in the tomato (or mushrooms) and soy sauce and cook for 2-3 minutes, stirring. Add the tempeh and serve at once with brown rice, noodles or cooked brown lentils.

SWEET AND SOUR TOFU STEAKS

Cooking time — 10-15 minutes
Marinading time — at least 1 hour   Serves 4-6

The zesty flavour of the marinade is absorbed by the tofu before it is barbecued or baked. Try your own variations of the marinade and remember, if you can marinade the tofu for half a day in the refrigerator, the flavour will be more pronounced

2 teaspoons freshly grated root ginger
8 fl oz/240ml pineapple or tomato juice
4 spring onions, chopped
2 cloves garlic, crushed
1 tablespoon apple cider vinegar
2 tablespoons tamari or shoyu sauce
2 teaspoons honey
1 lb/500g tofu
A little soy flour for coating
Oil for frying

Garnish
**Fresh pineapple chunks, tomato wedges and
parsley**

Mix the ginger, pineapple (or tomato) juice, spring onions, garlic, vinegar, tamari (or shoyu sauce) and honey together thoroughly.

Cut the tofu into 6 slices, then arrange on a plate or glass dish. (N.B.: do not use an aluminium sheet as this reacts with the marinade.)

Pour the marinade over the tofu steaks, then cover and allow to stand at least 1 hour. Halfway through the marinading time, turn the tofu steaks over so the top absorbs its share of the marinade.

Drain the tofu steaks, keeping any excess marinade. (This can be used later in stir-fried vegetable or rice dishes or to add zest to a basic soup recipe.)

Coat the steaks with the soya flour. Heat a barbecue or frying pan with a little oil and cook the steaks 5 minutes each side over moderate-high heat. Alternatively, brush a baking sheet or casserole dish with a little oil, then bake the steaks at 400°F, 200°C or Gas Mark 6 for 15 minutes. You may like to brush the excess marinade over the steaks for the last 5 minutes of baking.

Serve with steamed or fresh vegetables and a grain dish such as stir-fried rice or a tasty rice salad. Also delicious served cold as a sandwich filling.

SCRUMPTIOUS TEMPEH OR TOFU SATAY

Cooking time — 20 minutes   Serves 4

1 lb/500g tempeh or tofu, drained
About 4 tablespoons oil
1 onion, chopped
7½ oz/215g ground peanuts or 6 tablespoons peanut butter
¾ pint/425ml water
Pinch of chilli powder
1 tablespoon white miso or 2 teaspoons dark miso
1 tablespoon soy sauce

Cut the tempeh (or tofu) into ½ inch/1cm cubes and thread onto skewers. Heat the oil and fry the tempeh (or tofu) until golden brown.

Remove from the pan and drain well, keep hot in a 325°F, 170°C or Gas Mark 3 oven. Using about 2 tablespoons of the remaining oil, cook the onion and garlic for 2 minutes. Add the peanuts (or peanut butter), water and chilli powder and bring to the boil, stirring. Reduce the heat and cook the sauce gently until the desired consistency is reached — about 15 minutes. Blend the miso with a little sauce, then stir it into the remaining sauce with the soy sauce.

Place the tempeh (or tofu) on a bed of rice or wholemeal toast and spoon the sauce over. Serve with a colourful crispy salad.

SPECIAL CHILLI CON CARNE

Cooking time — 20 minutes   Serves 6

This is not only a high-protein dish, with the combination of kidney beans and TVP but it is also substantial, tasty and very satisfying

4 oz/115g TVP
8 fl oz/240ml boiling water
1-2 tablespoons oil
1 onion, chopped
1 pepper, chopped
1-2 cloves garlic
½ fresh chilli, chopped
or ½-1 level teaspoon chilli powder
4 tomatoes, chopped
2 tablespoons tomato purée
¾ pint/425ml water or vegetable stock
¾ pint/425ml cooked or canned red kidney beans

Place the TVP in a bowl and cover with boiling water.

Meanwhile, heat the oil gently and cook the onion, pepper, garlic and chilli (or chilli powder) for 2 minutes, stirring. Add the tomatoes and tomato purée and cook, stirring for 3 minutes. Add the water (or vegetable stock), TVP and red kidney beans and mix well.

Bring to the boil, stirring, then reduce the heat to a simmer. Cook gently for 15 minutes. Season to taste with salt and pepper and serve in taco shells with grated tasty cheese and shredded lettuce.

This can also be made into a delicious casserole by topping with grated cheese and browning it in the oven. Or simply serve it as a stew, accompanied by wholemeal bread and a leafy salad.

TOFU BOLOGNESE SAUCE

Cooking time — 20-25 minutes   Serves 4-6

This is a great way to use frozen, thawed tofu or home-made TVP as the texture is chewy and satisfying, especially suitable for those who are used to eating meat. Should you use fresh tofu, the texture will be much softer and the colour of the sauce much lighter

I tablespoon oil
2 onions, chopped finely
3 cloves garlic, crushed
I lb/500g tofu, drained well and chopped
I pepper, washed, seeded and chopped
4 ripe tomatoes, washed and chopped
3 tablespoons tomato purée
I tablespoon chopped fresh basil or 2 teaspoons dried basil
2 teaspoons chopped fresh oregano or I teaspoon dried oregano
¾ pint/425ml water or vegetable stock
A little salt and freshly ground black pepper to taste
Handful of parsley, chopped
7 oz/200g spaghetti

Heat the oil in a frying pan with the onions and garlic, tofu and chopped pepper and stir over low-moderate heat for 1-2 minutes. Add the tomatoes and tomato purée, sweet basil, oregano and water (or stock). Stir until the mixture reaches boiling point, then reduce heat and simmer gently for 20 minutes.

Cook the spaghetti or soyeroni in boiling water while the sauce is bubbling. Season sauce to taste with salt and black pepper and stir in the parsley. Serve over drained pasta.

LOAVES

Soya loaves are delicious served with baked vegetables and a tasty sauce. Left over or cold loaves also dress up salads and make great sandwich fillings.

SCRUMPTIOUS SOYA LOAF

Cooking time — 35-40 minutes   Makes 1 standard loaf

1 lb 2 oz/510g okara or cooked, ground soya beans
1½ medium carrots, scrubbed and grated
1 medium-large onion, grated
2 cloves garlic, crushed (optional)
1 ripe tomato, chopped
1 stick celery, finely chopped
2 tablespoons tamari or shoyu sauce
A little freshly ground black pepper or sweet
basil to taste
2 oz/55g soya flour
Small handful of freshly chopped parsley

Mix all the ingredients together thoroughly. Press down firmly into a lightly-oiled loaf tin and bake at 375°F, 190°C or Gas Mark 5 until firm and golden brown.

VARIATIONS

Substitute ½ pepper, finely chopped, for the celery.

Substitute 6 oz/170g steamed green peas or cauliflower or broccoli florets for the grated carrots.

Try lining the loaf tin with brown paper then brush with a little oil. Arrange a pattern of lightly steamed vegetable slices or fresh tomato slices on the bottom before filling the tin with the loaf mixture.

SPECIAL TEMPEH CASHEW LOAF

Cooking time — 50-55 minutes   Serves 6

13 oz/375g tempeh
5 oz/140g cashew nuts, chopped or ground
1 onion, chopped
2 tablespoons soy sauce
2 tablespoons tahini or 1-2 eggs, beaten
2 cloves garlic, crushed
2 tomatoes, chopped or 2 tablespoons tomato purée
1 lb/500g cooked brown rice or 6 oz/170g breadcrumbs
A little salt and freshly ground black pepper
A little oil

Mash the tempeh with a fork and mix in the cashews, onion, soy sauce, tahini (or eggs), garlic, tomatoes (or tomato purée), brown rice (or breadcrumbs), salt and freshly ground black pepper until well combined.

Lightly brush a loaf tin with oil, using a pastry brush and pack the mixture down into the tin.

Bake at 350°F, 180°C or Gas Mark 4 for 50-55 minutes.

Serve hot with instant miso sauce or cold as a sandwich filling.

VARIATIONS

Substitute 4 oz/100g chopped mushrooms for the two chopped tomatoes.

TEMPEH VEGETABLE LOAF

Cooking time — 45-50 minutes   Serves 6

Delicious both hot and cold

13 oz/375g tempeh
2 tablespoons soy sauce
2 tablespoons tahini or 2 eggs, beaten
1 carrot, scrubbed and grated
1 onion, chopped
Small handful parsley, chopped
2 cloves garlic, crushed
Pinch of dried, sweet basil
6 oz/170g breadcrumbs or ¾ lb/340g rice bran
A little oil

Mash the tempeh with a fork and mix thoroughly with soy sauce and tahini (or eggs). Add the carrot, onion, parsley, garlic, sweet basil and breadcrumbs (or rice bran) and mix thoroughly.

Lightly oil a loaf tin using a pastry brush. Pack the mixture down into the tin and bake at 350°F, 180°C or Gas Mark 4 for 45-50 minutes.

Serve hot or cold.

VARIATIONS

Try adding 1-2 sticks finely chopped celery or ½ finely chopped pepper.

Try adding 1 tablespoon curry powder to the mixture before placing in loaf tin.

BURGERS

Substantial, nutritious, delicious and versatile burgers can be precooked and stored in the refrigerator or freezer for 'instant' meals. Serve them cold for picnics and packed lunches or reheat them on a baking sheet in the oven at 400°F, 200°C or Gas Mark 6 for 10-15 minutes.

Burgers can be served in any way you choose. Try them in a wholemeal bun with chutney or salad or with hot baked or steamed vegetables.

Cooking

Burgers are usually fried until golden brown in a *little* oil. Soya food burger mixtures are usually low in fat and so using a little oil for cooking won't cause an excess of fat in your diet.

However, should you wish to omit the frying process, you may bake the burgers in the oven instead. Dab a little oil on a paper towel or tissue and rub it over a baking sheet or brush a little oil on the sheet with a pastry brush. Form the burger mixture into balls and then roll them in sesame seeds, wheatgerm or breadcrumbs. Place them on the baking sheet and bake at 400°F, 200°C or Gas Mark 6 for 20-25 minutes.

Burgers are also delicious barbecued.

SUPER SOYA BURGERS

Cooking time — 10 minutes   Makes about 12-15

This is an especially good way to use okara by replacing the cooked, ground soya beans with 1 lb 2 oz/510g okara. This recipe also makes good use of leftover cooked vegetables

1 lb 2 oz/510g canned or cooked soya beans or okara
5 oz/140g steamed vegetables (pumpkin, carrot
celery, cauliflower)
1 onion, finely chopped
1-2 cloves garlic, crushed (optional)
Small handful of parsley, chopped
1 tablespoon miso (white) or 2 tablespoons soy sauce
1 tablespoon tahini or 1 egg, beaten
Pinch of sweet basil
2 oz/55g soya flour
4 oz/115g bran or 2 oz/55g breadcrumbs
Oil for frying

Grind the soya beans in a food processor or mincer. Mash the vegetables and add to the soya beans (or okara) with the onion, garlic, parsley, miso (or soy sauce), tahini (or egg) and sweet basil.

Mix thoroughly then add the soya flour and bran (or breadcrumbs). Combine well and form into burgers. Fry until golden brown in a little oil.

TREMENDOUS TEMPEH BURGERS

Tempeh makes great burgers. Its firm beany texture means that the burgers bind well and as a bonus they develop a crispy surface when fried.

MUSHROOM BURGERS

Cooking time — 10 minutes   Makes about 12

13 oz/375g tempeh
1 onion, chopped
1-2 cloves garlic, crushed
5 oz/140g chopped mushrooms
2 tablespoons tahini or 1-2 eggs, beaten
2 teaspoons dark miso or 1 tablespoon white miso
Pinch of sweet basil

2-4 oz/55-115g cup soya flour
Oil for frying
Additional flour or rice bran for coating
burgers

Mash the tempeh with a fork and mix in the onion, garlic and chopped mushrooms. Mix in the tahini (or eggs), and miso.

Add the sweet basil and lastly the soya flour. Mix thoroughly. Form into burgers and coat with additional flour (or rice bran).

Fry until brown and serve in a bun with salad or with baked or steamed vegetables. Delicious hot or cold.

CARROT BURGERS

Cooking time — 5-10 minutes   Makes about 10-12

13 oz/375g tempeh
1 carrot, scrubbed and grated
2 tablespoons tahini or 1 egg, beaten
2 tablespoons soy sauce
½ bunch spring onions, chopped
Pinch of dried sweet basil
Freshly ground black pepper
1 tablespoon tomato purée (optional)
A little salt to taste
Oil for frying — about 1-2 tablespoons

Mash the tempeh with a fork and mix well with carrot, tahini (or egg), soy sauce, spring onions, sweet basil, black pepper, tomato purée and salt. Form into burgers. Allow to stand for 5 minutes if possible to allow burgers to become firm.

Heat the oil in a frying pan and cook the burgers over moderate-high heat until they are golden brown on both sides.

LUCKY LENTIL BURGERS

Cooking time — Lentils, 45 minutes
Burgers, 5-10 minutes   Makes about 12

13 oz/375g tempeh, mashed
1 lb/455g cooked brown lentils, well drained
2 tablespoons tahini or 1-2 eggs, beaten
1 tablespoon white miso or 2 teaspoons dark miso
1 onion, finely chopped
2 cloves garlic, crushed
Small handful parsley, chopped
A little salt and freshly ground black pepper
4 oz/115g breadcrumbs or ½ lb/225g rice bran
4 oz/115g soya flour
Oil for frying

Mix the tempeh, brown lentils, tahini (or eggs), miso, onion, garlic, parsley and salt and black pepper to taste. Add the breadcrumbs (or rice bran) and mix thoroughly.

Form into burgers and coat with soya flour. Fry until golden brown on both sides. Serve hot or cold.

TASTY TOFU BURGERS

Cooking time — 10 minutes   Makes about 12

These burgers can also be made from tempeh instead of tofu

1 lb/500g tofu, drained
1 onion, finely chopped
2 teaspoons freshly chopped sweet basil or ½-1 level
teaspoon dried sweet basil
1 medium carrot, scrubbed and grated
Small handful parsley, chopped
2 cloves garlic, crushed
1 tablespoon miso or soy sauce
2 tablespoons peanut butter
4 oz/115g fresh wholemeal breadcrumbs
Freshly ground black pepper to taste
Oil for frying
4 oz/115g soya flour

Place the tofu between 2 layers of paper towel or a clean tea towel and press any excess water out. Mash with a fork, or chop, then mix thoroughly with all the other ingredients. Form into burgers and coat with a thin layer of flour. Fry until golden brown on both sides.

TOFU AND CASHEW BURGERS

Cooking time — 15-20 minutes   Makes about 12

1 lb/500g tofu, drained
5 oz/140g dry roasted cashew pieces
1 onion, finely chopped
2 tablespoons tahini or 1-2 eggs, beaten
5 spring onions, chopped
A little salt and freshly ground black pepper
4 oz/115g fresh wholemeal breadcrumbs
1 tablespoon miso or soy sauce
5 oz/140g crushed cashews for coating burgers or,
if frying, 4 oz/115g soya flour

Place the tofu between 2 layers of paper towel or a clean tea towel and press any excess water out. Mash or chop, then mix thoroughly with the other ingredients.

Form into balls, then roll in crushed cashew nuts. Place on a lightly oiled baking sheet and bake at 400°F, 200°C or Gas Mark 6 until golden brown (about 15-20 minutes). Alternatively, form into burgers, coat lightly with flour, then fry in a little oil until golden brown each side.

CASSEROLES

Casseroles are ever popular as they are often 'one dish' meals. Try serving these favourites with fresh wholemeal bread or crusty rolls. As a texture contrast, serve with alfalfa sprouts or bean shoots.

SCRUMPTIOUS SOYA LAYER CASSEROLE

Cooking time — 40 minutes   Serves 6

A little oil
½ bunch spring onions, chopped
Pinch of sweet basil
2 cloves garlic, crushed
3 ripe tomatoes, chopped or 5 oz/125g
mushrooms, sliced
8 fl oz/240ml vegetable stock or water
½ lb/225g soya grits
I tablespoon soy sauce
I lb 6 oz/625g well cooked soya beans or canned
soya beans
I bunch spinach, washed and chopped
4 oz/115g grated tasty cheese or 5 oz/140g cashew nut
pieces
Freshly chopped parsley

Heat the oil and cook spring onions, basil and garlic gently for I minute. Stir in the tomatoes (or mushrooms) and stir over moderate heat for 2 minutes. Add the vegetable stock (or water) and bring to the boil, stirring. Reduce the heat to a simmer then cook gently for 10 minutes.

Stir in the soya grits and soy sauce. Place half the spinach in a casserole dish then top with ¾ lb/340g of cooked soya beans. Pour half the tomato or mushroom sauce over the beans then top with 2 oz/55g grated cheese (or 2½ oz/70g cashews).

Add the remaining spinach and press down. Repeat layers and bake at 350°F, 180°C or Gas Mark 4 until golden brown.

'MEATY' MEATLESS MOUSSAKA

Cooking time — 50-55 minutes   Serves 4-6

2 tablespoons oil
1 onion, chopped
2 cloves garlic, crushed
½ lb/225g TVP soaked in 15 fl oz/425ml boiling water
for 15 minutes or 1½ lbs/680g prefrozen, chopped
tofu
2 medium aubergines, cut into ¼ inch/5mm slices
4 medium tomatoes, cut into ¼ inch/5mm slices
Salt and freshly ground black pepper to taste
4 oz/115g grated tasty cheese (optional)

Put the aubergine slices on a baking sheet and bake at 400°F, 200°C or Gas Mark 6 for 15 minutes.

Meanwhile, heat the oil and cook the onion and garlic gently for 2 minutes. Add the TVP (or tofu) and stir over moderate heat for 10 minutes. Brush a little oil around the inside of a casserole dish, then arrange alternate layers of aubergine slices, tomato and TVP, ending with a layer of tomato. Top with the grated tasty cheese and bake, covered, at 350°F, 180°C or Gas Mark 4 for about 30 minutes. Remove the cover and continue cooking at 400°F, 200°C or Gas Mark 6 for another 10 minutes.

TOFU & VEGETABLE CASSEROLE

Cooking time — 20-25 minutes   Serves 6

4 medium sized potatoes, scrubbed
1-2 tablespoons oil
1 large onion, chopped
2 cloves garlic, crushed
1 pepper, chopped
4 ripe tomatoes, cut into wedges
A little salt and freshly ground black pepper
to taste
1 lb/500g tofu, drained, mashed

Topping:
2 oz (55g) fresh wholemeal breadcrumbs or bran
½-1 tablespoon sesame seeds
½ teaspoon sweet paprika
1-2 tablespoons oil

Steam the potatoes until tender, about 20 minutes. Meanwhile, heat the oil and cook the onion, garlic and pepper over low-moderate heat for 2-3 minutes. Stir in the tomatoes, vegetable salt and black pepper and cook, stirring for 1 minute. Stir in the tofu.

Cut the potatoes in ¼ inch/5mm slices and arrange on the base and sides of a lightly oiled casserole dish. Top with the tomato/tofu mixture.

Mix the breadcrumbs (or bran), sesame seeds, sweet paprika and oil (it's best to use your hands for thorough mixing). Sprinkle the mixture on top of the tomatoes, then bake at 400°F, 200°C or Gas Mark 6 for 15 minutes. Sprinkle with freshly chopped parsley and serve piping hot.

VARIATIONS

Try adding 6 oz/170g cooked soya beans, brown lentils or red kidney beans to the tofu/tomato mixture before baking.

Use slices of steamed pumpkin, sweet potato or courgette instead of potatoes.

TOFU AND SPINACH QUICHE

Cooking time — Pastry, 10 minutes   Quiche, 25 minutes
For a 9½ inch/24cm quiche tin

A quick and easy way to make a quiche without eggs. If you include cheese in your diet you may like to sprinkle the quiche with grated tasty cheese before baking

Pastry

Use half the quantity of Tofu pastry (see page 104) to line the base of the quiche tin. Bake at 400°F, 200°C or Gas Mark 6 for 10 minutes. Meanwhile prepare the filling.

Filling

I lb/500g tofu
8 fl oz/240ml soya milk
I tablespoon fresh dill, chopped or 2 teaspoons dried dill
3 tablespoons tahini
2 tablespoons tamari or shoyu sauce
2 cloves garlic, crushed
½ bunch spinach, well-washed and dried
I onion, finely chopped
3 ripe tomatoes, sliced

Blend the tofu, soya milk, dill, tahini, tamari (or shoyu sauce) and garlic until smooth. Mix the spinach with the onion, then mix through the tofu mixture. Place in the partly cooked pastry case and pat down flat.

Bake at 400°F, 200°C or Gas Mark 6 for 25 minutes. Top with fresh tomato slices and serve hot or cold with a crispy salad.

SAVOURY PUMPKIN PIE

Cooking time — Filling, 15 minutes   Pie, 25-30 minutes
For a 9½ inch/24cm quiche or flan tin

A colourful and tasty pie. It's best to prepare the filling beforehand and use it when it's cool. This will help retain the crispness of the pastry

Pastry

Use 1 quantity of Tofu pastry (see page 83). Roll it out and line the tin with half the pastry. Moisten the edges with a little water.

Filling
2 lbs 3 oz/1kg pumpkin, chopped into cubes
1 onion, chopped
6 oz/170g green peas or ½ lb/225g green beans (cut into ½ inch/1cm pieces)
9-13 oz/250-375g tofu, mashed
1 teaspoon ground cumin
A little salt and freshly ground black pepper
to taste
Small handful chopped parsley or chopped
spinach

Steam the pumpkin, onion and peas (or beans) until tender — about 15 minutes. Cool. Mix the tofu, cumin, vegetable salt, black pepper and parsley (or spinach) until well combined. Mix the pumpkin, onion and peas (or beans) with the tofu. Place in the pastry case.

Roll out the other half of the pastry and arrange on top. Press the edges together to seal them, then trim off the excess pastry. Pinch the edges in a fluted design, then bake the pie at 400°F, 200°C or Gas Mark 6 in the hottest part of the oven for 30 minutes.

Serve hot or cold. This pie also reheats very well.

TASTY TEMPEH PIZZA

Cooking time — 25-30 minutes   For a 9½ inch/24cm pizza tin

The tempeh adds taste and texture to a favourite recipe, making this a satisfying one-dish meal

Crust
Use this recipe for the crust or substitute with a Tofu pastry (see page 83)
6 oz/170g wholemeal self-raising flour
Pinch of oregano
2 tablespoons melted butter
1-2 tablespoons oil
About 4 fl oz/115ml water or milk

Mix the flour and oregano, then add the butter, oil and water (or milk). Mix well to form a soft dough, then knead for a few seconds.

Roll out to about ¼ inch/5mm thickness and line a pizza tin or flan or quiche tin. Trim the edges. Bake at 400°F, 200°C or Gas Mark 6 for 10 minutes.

Topping
A little oil (about 1 tablespoon)
½ onion, chopped
½ pepper, chopped
1 clove garlic, crushed
Pinch of sweet basil
2-3 ripe tomatoes, chopped
4 tablespoons water
4 oz/115g grated tasty cheese (optional)
½ packet tempeh (about 5¾ oz/160g) chopped
2 oz/55g sliced mushrooms
2 tablespoons sliced olives
2 oz/55g chopped pineapple (optional)

Heat the oil in a frying pan and cook the onion, pepper and garlic for 1 minute, stirring. Stir in the tomatoes and basil and continue to cook for 2 minutes. Add the water and cook for 5 minutes, stirring. Continue to cook until a thick sauce is obtained. Cool.

Spread the sauce over the precooked crust and top with the cheese, then the tempeh, mushrooms, olives and pineapple.

Cook at 425°F, 220°C or Gas Mark 7 for 20-25 minutes or until golden brown. Serve at once with a crispy salad.

HURRY CURRY TEMPEH

Cooking time — 20-25 minutes   Serves 6

A colourful and tasty dish which is surprisingly satisfying

1-2 tablespoons oil
9 oz/250g tempeh, cut into ½ inch/1cm cubes
1 onion, chopped
1-2 cloves garlic, crushed
1-1½ tablespoons curry powder
15 fl oz/425ml of tomato juice or vegetable stock
¾ lb/340g pumpkin or carrot, cut into ½ inch/1cm cubes
6 oz/170g peas
½ lb/225g cauliflower or broccoli florets
A little salt and freshly ground black pepper
A little chopped parsley

For a special touch
6 tablespoons yoghurt
A little red pepper, finely chopped
A little spring onion, finely chopped

Heat the oil and cook the tempeh until golden brown. Remove the tempeh and add the onion, garlic and curry powder and cook gently, stirring for a few minutes. Add the tomato juice (or vegetable stock) and bring to the boil, stirring.

Stir in the pumpkin (or carrot) and peas, then reduce the heat to a gentle simmer and cook for 10 minutes. Stir in the cauliflower (or broccoli) and cook gently for 5-10 minutes only. Season with salt and pepper and stir in the parsley and tempeh.

Serve piping hot with rice or wholemeal toast. For a special touch, at the last minute top each serving of the curry with 1 tablespoon of yoghurt, then sprinkle with chopped red pepper and spring onion.

Note: This is doubly delicious cooked the day before you want to use it. Store it in the refrigerator overnight, then reheat it gently. Take care not to overcook when reheating.

SOYA-STUFFED PEPPERS

Cooking time — 25-30 minutes   Serves 6

6 medium sized peppers
I tablespoon oil
I onion, finely chopped
I-2 cloves garlic, crushed
I ripe tomato, sliced
2½ oz/70g mushrooms, sliced
¾ lb/340g cooked or canned soya beans or okara
I tablespoon soy sauce
½ teaspoon dried sweet basil
Handful of chopped parsley
Freshly ground black pepper
2 oz/55g wholemeal breadcrumbs or 6 oz/170g cooked
brown rice

Steam the peppers for 5 minutes. Cool. Meanwhile heat the oil and cook the onion and garlic over a moderate heat for a few minutes. Add the tomato and mushrooms and cook, stirring for 5 minutes. Add the soya beans (or okara), soy sauce, sweet basil, parsley and freshly ground black pepper. Mix thoroughly, then stir in the breadcrumbs (or rice).

Remove the tops and seeds from the peppers then fill with the above mixture. Place in a lightly oiled casserole dish and cover with the lid or foil.

Bake at 350°F, 180°C or Gas Mark 4 for 20 minutes. Remove the lid or foil for the last 5 minutes of cooking time.

VARIATIONS

Try adding 2 oz/55g grated tasty cheese to the filling and then sprinkle the peppers with a little Parmesan cheese before baking. Dust with a little sweet paprika before serving.

CHAPTER FOUR

SALADS AND
ACCOMPANIMENTS

TASTY SOY SALAD

Serves 4-6

Substantial and nutritious, this makes a satisfying light meal when accompanied by wholemeal bread and a leafy salad. It also keeps well in the refrigerator for about 2 days

¾ lb/340g cooked or canned soya beans
3 spring onions, chopped
Squeeze of lemon juice
1 tablespoon soy sauce
1 teaspoon honey
1 clove garlic, crushed
½ red pepper, chopped
1 stick celery, chopped
2 ripe tomatoes, chopped
Small handful parsley, chopped
Handful of bean shoots

Mix the soya beans, spring onions, lemon juice, soy sauce, honey and garlic and allow to stand for 30 minutes if possible, to allow absorption of flavours.

Carefully mix in the pepper, celery, tomatoes, parsley and bean shoots and serve in crisp lettuce cups.

Right: Scrumptious Soya Loaf (page 49) is delicious with baked vegetables and a tasty sauce while Soya-stuffed Peppers (page 63) in the foreground make an equally delicious dish for a main course
Overleaf, left: Tofu Mayonnaise (page 70) makes an excellent accompaniment to a crisp Golden Spinach and Tofu Salad (page 65)

GOLDEN SPINACH AND TOFU SALAD

Serves 4

Refreshingly tangy, this is a vitality-packed lunchbox treat or a great salad accompaniment for a hot, spicy main meal

9 oz/250g tofu, cut into ½ inch/1cm cubes
¼ of a fresh, ripe pineapple cut into ½ inch/1cm cubes
1½ oz/45g sultanas or raisins
1 teaspoon honey
1 tablespoon lemon juice
Handful shredded spinach

Dressing
9 oz/250g tofu
1 teaspoon honey
8 fl oz/240ml fruit juice (apple or pineapple)
2 tablespoons tahini
Roasted cashews for decoration

Carefully mix the tofu, pineapple, sultanas (or raisins), honey, lemon juice and spinach. Blend the dressing ingredients together well.

Just before serving, place a generous dollop of dressing on each serving of salad and sprinkle with a few roasted cashews.

Previous page, right: Creamy Tofu Ice-cream (page 77) makes a refreshing change from milk-based ice-creams and is a boon for those on a low-calorie diet or allergic to cow's milk
Left: Delight your family and friends with Creamy Carob Cheesecake (page 75) as a scrumptious end to a meal

TEMPTING TEMPEH SALAD

Serves 4

This is a delicious light meal with a wholemeal roll or a tasty accompaniment for casseroles and curries

About 6 oz/175g tempeh
1 tablespoon soy sauce
2 handfuls of bean shoots
4 spring onions, chopped
1 stick celery, chopped
4 oz/115g chopped pineapple (optional)

Steam the tempeh for 10 minutes, then cool. Cut into cubes or strips, sprinkle with the soy sauce, then mix with the bean shoots, spring onions and celery.
Add the pineapple for a special treat. Serve in lettuce cups.

CASHEW AND TEMPEH SALAD

Cooking time — 10-15 minutes   Serves 4-6

A protein-packed dish, this is a particulary good lunchbox treat

6-8 oz/170-225g tempeh
A little oil
4 spring onions, chopped
1 red apple, diced
1½ oz/45g sultana or 3 oz/85g grapes
1 teaspoon honey
Squeeze of lemon juice
2 oz/55g dry-roasted cashews

Place the tempeh on a baking sheet and brush with a little oil. Bake at 425°F, 220°C or Gas Mark 7 for 15 minutes. Alternatively, steam the tempeh for 10 minutes (steaming will produce a softer texture while baking will give a crunchy texture). Cool the tempeh and cut into strips or cubes. Combine with the spring onions, apple, and sultanas (or grapes).
Mix the honey and lemon juice in a cup and mix through the salad just before serving. Sprinkle the cashews on top and serve.

TOFU AND SPROUT SALAD

Serves 4

This is a basic recipe using tofu marinaded in tamari or shoyu sauce. Try adding
the marinaded tofu to any of your favourite salads — Greek salad for example
can be made with tofu instead of feta cheese

9 oz/250g tofu, chopped into ½ inch/1cm cubes
1 tablespoon tamari or shoyu sauce
Squeeze of lemon juice
2 tablespoons olive oil
1 teaspoon honey
2 handfuls bean shoots
Freshly ground black pepper
1 stick celery, finely sliced

Place the tofu cubes in a bowl and sprinkle with the tamari (or shoyu sauce).
Squeeze the lemon over the tofu and dribble the oil and honey over.

Mix carefully to avoid breaking up the tofu. Allow to stand 15 minutes at least,
then add the sprouts, black pepper and celery. Mix lightly and serve in crisp lettuce
cups.

BAKED JACKET POTATOES WITH TOFU

Cooking time — 45 minutes   Makes 6

6 medium sized old potatoes, scrubbed
A little salt (optional)
9 oz/250g tofu
8 fl oz/240ml yoghurt or 7 fl oz/200ml soya milk
1 tablespoon snipped chives
Sweet paprika

Rub a little salt onto each potato if liked. Place the potatoes on a baking sheet.
Cut a cross ½ inch/1cm into the top of each potato. Bake at 375°F, 190°C or
Gas Mark 5 for 45 minutes or until tender.

Meanwhile, blend the tofu with the yoghurt (or soya milk), stir in the chives.

When the potatoes are ready, press them firmly in at the sides to open up
the top. Place a dollop of the tofu mixture on each potato and dust with paprika.
Serve at once.

SOYA SAVOURY

Cooking time — 35 minutes

A scrumptious snack or party nibble or an unusual topping for thick vegetable soup. Also try adding it to your favourite savoury salad instead of nuts

1 lb 2 oz/610g cooked, canned or sprouted soya beans
1 tablespoon soy sauce
1 tablespoon honey
¼ teaspoon sea salt
A little oil

If using cooked or canned beans, drain them well.

Mix the beans, soy sauce, honey and salt well. Spread out in a thin layer on a baking sheet which has been brushed with a little oil.

Bake at 400°F, 200°C or Gas Mark 6 until golden brown, about 35 minutes. Cool to obtain a crunchy texture. When completely cold store in an airtight jar.

VARIATION

Mix with 5 oz/140g roasted nuts and sunflower seeds for a nutritious snack or party nibble.

CAULIFLOWER AND TOFU BAKE

Cooking time — 35 minutes   Serves 4-6

For those who don't include dairy products in their diet, but sadly miss cauliflower cheese, this is a treat. An added bonus is its low-calorie content. For cheese lovers, top with 2 oz/55g grated tasty cheese before baking

½ large or 1 small cauliflower, trimmed and
washed
13 oz/375g tofu
1 tablespoon oil
12 fl oz/340ml soya milk
A little salt and freshly ground black pepper
to taste
1 clove garlic, chopped
6 spring onions, chopped
1½ tablespoons sesame seeds or ground almonds
Sweet paprika

Cut or break the cauliflower into florets and cut the stalks into ¾ inch/2cm chunks. Steam the florets and stalks until tender, about 10-15 minutes, then arrange them in a lightly oiled casserole dish.

Blend the tofu, oil, milk, salt and pepper, garlic and spring onions well. Pour the mixture over the cauliflower, then sprinkle with the sesame seeds (or ground almonds).

Bake at 400°F, 200°C or Gas Mark 6 until golden, about 20 minutes. Dust with sweet paprika and serve at once with steamed or baked vegetables and some leafy greens.

TOFU POTATO PATTIES

Cooking time — 10 minutes   Makes about 12

3 medium potatoes, cooked
9 oz/250g tofu
8 fl oz/240ml soya milk
1 onion, finely chopped
A little salt and finely ground black pepper to
taste
4 oz/115g soya flour
Additional 2-4 oz/55-115g soya flour for coating pasties
Oil for frying, about 2 tablespoons

Mash the potatoes and tofu with a fork. Mix in the soya milk, onion and salt and pepper and then add the soya flour. Form into patties and coat with soya flour.

Heat the oil in a frying pan and fry patties for 3-5 minutes each side until golden brown. Serve hot.

VARIATIONS

Use 2 potatoes and add 3 oz/85g cooked green peas or any other left over cooked vegetables.

TEMPEH TOMATOES
Serves 6

About 6 oz/175g tempeh
A little olive oil for frying
4 spring onions, chopped
1 clove garlic, crushed
2 teaspoons soy sauce
A little chopped sweet basil
6 large tomatoes, washed

Heat the oil in a frying pan and fry the slab of tempeh until golden brown on both sides. Drain well. Chop the tempeh and combine it with the spring onions, garlic, soy sauce and sweet basil.

Cut the tops off the tomatoes and, using a teaspoon, carefully scoop out the flesh. Chop the flesh well and drain any excess juice into your stock pot. Combine the chopped tomato flesh with the tempeh mixture and use to stuff the tomato shells.

Serve cold on a bed of greens or heat, covered, in a casserole at 350°F, 180°C or Gas Mark 4 for 20 minutes.

TOFU MAYONNAISE

This can be made in an instant just before you need it. Otherwise store it in a closed container for 4 or 5 days in the refrigerator

9 oz/250g tofu
8 fl oz/240ml soya milk
1 tablespoon lemon juice
½ teaspoon mustard
½ teaspoon salt
1 teaspoon honey
1 tablespoon vegetable oil
1 clove garlic, crushed (optional) or a few
snipped chives (optional)

Blend all the ingredients together well. For a thinner consistency, blend in a little more soya milk.

INSTANT MISO SAUCE

This sauce is so quick and easy to prepare that it can be a last minute addition to any meal. I've found it particularly handy when serving rice or pasta dishes or baked vegetables; instant miso sauce adds the bitey taste and moisture that these foods need

1½ tablespoons white or soba miso or 3 teaspoons mugi or
kome miso
2-3 tablespoons tahini
A little finely chopped parsley or favourite
herb
1 finely chopped spring onion or snipped
chives
8 fl oz/240ml boiling water
Freshly ground black pepper

Blend all the ingredients together well and serve at once. If reheating, take care to heat gently and do not boil.

VARIATION

Try adding 2 oz/55g chopped mushrooms or 1 ripe tomato, chopped.

CREAMY WHITE SAUCE

Cooking time — 5 minutes   *Makes ¾ pint/425ml*

A low-fat cholesterol-free sauce for use in your favourite recipes

1-2 tablespoons margarine
2 tablespoons white flour or 3 tablespoons soya flour
12 fl oz/340ml soya milk
Pinch of salt

Melt the margarine in a small saucepan and stir in the flour. Stir over a low heat for 1 minute. Stirring all the time, add the soya milk and bring to the boil. Reduce the heat to a simmer and cook another minute, still stirring.

VARIATION

To make thick white sauce for use in croquettes, use only 8 fl oz/240ml soya milk.

CREAMY MUSHROOM SAUCE

Cooking time — 10 minutes   Makes 1 pint/570ml

Great served with burgers, pies or filo rolls

1-2 tablespoons margarine or oil
½ small onion, finely chopped
3 oz/85g chopped mushrooms
3 tablespoons soya flour
8 fl oz/240ml soya milk
4 fl oz/115ml vegetable stock
A little salt and freshly ground black pepper
to taste

Heat the margarine (or oil) in a medium sized saucepan and add the chopped onion. Cook, stirring for 1 minute, then add the mushrooms. Stir over a moderate heat for 2-3 minutes, then stir in the soya flour.

Add the soya milk and vegetable stock and stir until boiling. Reduce the heat to a simmer and cook another minute.

CHAPTER FIVE

DESSERTS, CAKES AND MUNCHIES

TOFU CREAM

A delicious whipped cream substitute

8¾ oz/250g tofu
1 tablespoon honey
1 teaspoon vanilla essence
1 tablespoon carob powder (optional)

Blend all together well until velvety smooth. Place in piping bag and use to decorate cheesecakes, cakes, pancakes or desserts.

Tofu cream should be stored in the refrigerator and keeps for about 3 days.

CHEESECAKE BONANZAS

Being a fresh, soft cheese, tofu can be used in any cheesecake recipe to replace cream, cottage or Ricotta cheese. You can use any of your favourite recipes substituting the cheese with tofu or try the following

SPECIAL BAKED CHEESECAKE

Cooking time — 35-40 minutes
For a 9½ inch/24cm quiche or flan tin or a 8 inch/20cm springform tin

I tablespoon honey
I tablespoon fruit juice
I tablespoon oil
1½ oz/45g desiccated coconut or ground almonds
2 oz/55g soya flour
4 oz/115g oats

Mix the honey, fruit juice and oil. Mix the desiccated coconut (or ground almonds), soya flour and rolled oats, then add the liquid ingredients, rubbing them through with your fingertips. Pat the crust onto the base of the lightly oiled tin.

Filling
I lb/500g tofu
15 fl oz/425ml soya milk
I teaspoon vanilla essence
2-3 tablespoons honey
3 oz/85g raisins or sultanas
Lightly stewed apple slices for decoration
Ground cinnamon

Blend the tofu, soya milk, vanilla and honey until smooth. Sprinkle the raisins (or sultanas) over the crust, then pour the tofu mixture on top. Bake at 375°F, 190°C or Gas Mark 5 until set (about 30-35 minutes). However, if you use the 8 inch/20cm springform tin, the filling will take longer to cook in the middle. In this case you will need to cook the cheesecake for an additional 10-15 minutes.

Turn the oven off and leave the cheesecake in the oven to cool if possible. (This will help prevent cracking.) Chill in the refrigerator. Decorate with stewed apple slices and dust with cinnamon or top with slices of fresh fruit in season.

CREAMY CAROB CHEESECAKE

Cooking time — Crust, 15 minutes   Cheesecake, 30-45 minutes
For a 9½ inch/24cm quiche or flan tin or an 8 inch/20cm springform pan

Crust
3 oz/85g desiccated coconut or ground almonds
1 tablespoon carob powder
2 oz/55g wholemeal flour or soya flour
2 oz/55g rolled oats
2 tablespoons oil
1 tablespoon honey
2 tablespoons soya milk or water

Mix the desiccated coconut (or ground almonds), carob powder, wholemeal (or soya) flour and oats. Mix the oil, honey and soya milk (or water) and combine thoroughly with the dry ingredients. Pat down the crust onto the bottom of the flan or springform tin which has been brushed lightly with oil. Bake at 375°F, 190°C or Gas Mark 5 for 15 minutes.

Filling
1 lb/500g tofu
3 tablespoons carob powder
3 tablespoons honey
4-8 fl oz/115-240ml soya milk
1 tablespoon vanilla essence
3 tablespoons coconut cream
Tofu cream (see page 73)
Fresh strawberries or pecan nuts

Blend all the filling ingredients together until very smooth. Pour on top of the precooked crust and bake at 375°F, 190°C or Gas Mark 5 until set — about 30 minutes if using a flan tin and up to 45 minutes if using a springform tin.

Turn off the heat and allow the cheesecake to cool in the oven if possible. Chill in the refrigerator, then decorate with Tofu cream and fresh strawberries (or pecan nuts).

FRUITY BANANA SLICE

Cooking time — 20 minutes   For an 8 inch/20cm square shallow baking tin

6 oz/170g wholemeal flour
3 tablespoons soya flour
I teaspoon ground cinnamon
2 oz/55g ground almonds or desiccated coconut
I tablespoon raw cane sugar
2 tablespoons oil
I tablespoon honey
I tablespoon water

Mix the wholemeal flour, soya flour, cinnamon, ground almonds (or desiccated coconut) and sugar. Mix the oil and honey and work into the dry ingredients with water.

Press down onto the base of the baking tin which you should lightly oil beforehand. Bake at 375°F, 190°C or Gas Mark 5 for 15-20 minutes. Cool.

Filling
8 fl oz/240ml apple juice
I teaspoon agar agar powder
I lb/500g tofu
3 ripe bananas
1-2 tablespoons honey
Squeeze of lemon juice
Sliced kiwi fruit and strawberries or
passionfruit pulp

Place the apple juice and agar agar powder in a small saucepan and bring to the boil, stirring. Reduce the heat to a simmer and cook, stirring, until the agar agar is dissolved. Cool slightly.

Meanwhile, blend the tofu, bananas, honey and lemon juice until smooth. While the blender is operating, add the slightly cooled agar agar mixture, blending until the mixture is velvety smooth. Quickly pour the mixture on top of the crust and smooth the surface. Chill in the refrigerator.

Decorate with slices of kiwi fruit and strawberries (or top with some passionfruit pulp). Also delicious with Tofu cream (see page 73).

SUPER SOYA ICE-CREAMS

Home-made ice-cream often sets solid in the freezer because it has not been aerated to the extent of commercial ice-cream.

I usually remove it from the freezer 1 hour before use as this allows it to soften slightly.

If you are lucky enough to have an electric ice-cream maker, you will be able to make ice-cream with a fluffy texture.

Note: These ice-creams are relatively low in fat and calories and contain no cholesterol.

CREAMY TOFU ICE-CREAM

Makes 2½ pints/1.5l

¾ pint plus 6 tablespoons/500ml soya milk
5 tablespoons raw cane sugar
2 level teaspoons agar agar powder
13 oz/375g tofu
2 teaspoons vanilla essence
8 fl oz/240ml vegetable oil ('low flavoured' soya, grape seed, safflower)
¾ pint plus 6 tablespoons/500ml soya milk or fruit juice for rewhipping

Put ¾ pint plus 6 tablespoons/500ml of soya milk and the raw cane sugar in a medium saucepan. Sprinkle the agar agar powder on top. Stirring all the time, bring the milk to the boil, then reduce the heat to a simmer and cook for 1 minute. Stir in the mashed tofu and allow to cool slightly for about 10 minutes.

Blend the warm mixture until velvety smooth with the vanilla essence and oil. Pour into a container, cover and freeze overnight. Next morning, rewhip with the additional soya milk (or fruit juice) and refreeze.

Note: If the ice-cream has set in a hard block, you will need to chop it up roughly with a large knife or chopper before blending.

ICE-CREAM VARIATIONS

Soft scoop tofu ice-cream

After whipping with the additional soya milk (or fruit juice), serve at once.

Yummy honey ice-cream

Use 3-4 tablespoons honey instead of the raw cane sugar and omit the vanilla essence. I suggest using a 'low flavoured' honey such as clover or wildflower. The stronger flavoured honeys tend to overpower the other ingredients.

Banana bonanza ice-cream

When rewhipping, blend in 4-5 very ripe bananas and only 9 fl oz/250ml soya milk before refreezing.

'Caramel' ice-cream

Use only 3 tablespoons of the raw cane sugar and add 6 oz/170g chopped, dates to the soya milk before bringing to the boil.

SUPER SOYA PLUM PUDDING

Cooking time — 1 hour   For a 6 inch/16cm pudding bowl

6 oz/170g okara or cooked soya beans
8 fl oz/240ml stewed, puréed plums or apple
purée
1½ lbs/680g mixed dried fruit
1 tablespoon mixed spice
2 tablespoons tahini or 1 egg, beaten
1 tablespoon honey
9 oz/250g tofu
2 oz/55g fresh wholemeal breadcrumbs or 6 oz/170g
cooked rice
4 oz/115g soya flour

Mix the okara (or soya beans), plum (or apple) purée, mixed dried fruit, mixed spice, tahini (or egg) and the honey. Allow to stand for 1 hour. Mash the tofu well with a fork and stir into the mixture. Stir in the breadcrumbs (or rice) and the soya flour and place in well oiled pudding basin.

Cover with a cloth or lid and place in a large saucepan with ¾ inch/2cm water in the bottom. Cover the saucepan with a lid and bring the water to the boil.

Reduce the heat to a simmer and cook for 1 hour. Turn off the heat and allow to cool. Keep for 1 day before serving cold or reheat the pudding for 30 minutes in a saucepan of water as before.

MOIST AND NUTTY CARROT CAKE

Cooking time — 40-45 minutes   For an 8 inch/20cm square cake tin

Delicious and nutritious, this cake stays moist because of its honey and tofu content. Using soya flour also produces a cake with a 'soft crumb'

1 lb 2 oz/610g finely grated carrot
3 tablespoons honey
8 fl oz/240ml soya milk or water
2 tablespoons oil
8¾ oz/250g tofu
2 teaspoons cinnamon
1 teaspoon mixed spice
5 oz/140g chopped pecan nuts or walnuts
6 oz/170g sultanas
4 oz/115g wholemeal self-raising flour
1 oz/30g soya flour

Blend the carrot, honey, soya milk (or water), oil and tofu until well combined. Mix the cinnamon, mixed spice, nuts, sultanas and flours, then pour in the carrot mixture. Mix thoroughly.

Pour into a lightly oiled cake tin and bake at 350°F, 180°C or Gas Mark 4 until it is cooked throughout — about 40 minutes. (Test with a skewer to check if the middle is cooked: if the skewer comes out clean, it is ready; if some mixture clings to the skewer, leave it to cook a little longer and test again). Serve hot or cold.

APPLE AND SULTANA SLICE

Cooking time — 40 minutes   For an 8 inch/20cm square cake tin

Moist and fruity, this cake keeps well if you don't eat it first! And the flavour actually improves the next day

4 apples, washed and grated
1 teaspoon cinnamon
6 oz/170g sultanas
8¾ oz/250g tofu, mashed
3 oz/85g raw cane sugar
1 tablespoon honey
8 fl oz/240ml soya milk
½ lb/225g muesli
4 oz/115g wholemeal self-raising flour
4¼ oz/125g butter or margarine, melted
A little oil

Mix all the ingredients (except the oil) together well. Brush a little oil on the base and sides of the cake tin. Tip the cake mixture into the tin and pat down smooth with moistened hands. (This will help make a flat top.)

Bake at 400°F, 200°C or Gas Mark 6 for 40 minutes. Leave in the cake tin for 10 minutes then turn out.

Serve hot with Super soy ice-cream or cool and cut into slices.

BLUEBERRY MUFFINS

Cooking time — 20 minutes   Makes 12

9 oz/250g tofu, mashed
2 tablespoons soya-bean or grapeseed oil
2 tablespoons raw cane sugar
8 fl oz/240ml soya milk
1 punnet blueberries or blackcurrants, washed
4-6 oz/115-170g wholemeal self-raising flour
A little oil or melted butter or margarine

Mix the tofu, oil, raw cane sugar and soya milk. Stir in the blueberries (or blackcurrants) carefully. Add enough flour to bring to a thick batter consistency.

Brush the muffin tins with a little oil (or melted butter or margarine) and spoon the mixture in, allowing room for the muffins to rise.

Bake at 400°F, 200°C or Gas Mark 6 until golden brown and cooked through.

ALMOND SLICE

Cooking time — 35 minutes   For an 8 inch/20cm square cake tin

½ lb/225g toasted muesli
3 oz/85g desiccated coconut
4 oz/115g wholemeal self-raising flour
4 oz/115g almonds
3 tablespoons cocoa or carob powder
A little oil
9 oz/250g tofu, mashed
3 oz/85g raw cane sugar
1 tablespoon honey
4 oz/125g butter or margarine, melted
2 eggs, beaten
4 fl oz/115ml soya milk

Mix the muesli, coconut, flour and almonds. Add the remaining ingredients in the order given and mix all together thoroughly.

Place in the cake tin and pat down flat using moistened hands. Bake at 375°F, 190°C or Gas Mark 5 for 35 minutes. Cool in the tin then cut into slices.

SPICY APPLE PANCAKES

Cooking time — 5-10 minutes   Makes about 12

4 oz/115g wholemeal self-raising flour or 6 oz/170g
of cooked brown rice
2 oz/55g soya flour
2 oz/55g rice bran (optional)
1 grated apple
1 egg
8 fl oz/240ml soya milk
½ teaspoon cinnamon
1 tablespoon honey
Butter, oil or margarine for cooking

Blend all the ingredients together well and leave the mixture to stand for 10 minutes to allow it to thicken. Heat the butter (or oil or margarine) in a frying pan and fry large spoonfuls of the mixture until golden brown each side. Serve hot with stewed fruit, honey or pure maple syrup as a substantial dessert or breakfast.

TERRIFIC TOFU PANCAKES

Standing time — 30 minutes
Cooking time — 1 minute each side   Makes about 12

Try serving these in stacks with genuine maple syrup and Tofu cream or spread with butter or margarine and honey or jam

1 oz/30g soya flour
5 oz/140g wholemeal self-raising flour
1 tablespoon oil
6 oz/170g tofu
8 fl oz/240ml soya milk or ½ soya milk and ½ water
1 tablespoon honey
Few drops of vanilla essence
Oil for cooking

Blend all the ingredients together well for about 30 seconds. Allow to stand for 30 minutes if possible, to allow the starch in the flour to soften. This will also allow the mixture to thicken. Should it become too thick, thin down to a thick pouring custard consistency, using a little extra soya milk or water.

Heat a little oil in a frying pan and cook the mixture in tablespoonfuls until bubbles appear on the surface. Flip over and cook 1 minute on the other side. Lift out onto a tea towel and serve at once or cover and allow to cool.

TOFU PASTRY

For the top and bottom of a 9½ inch/24cm quiche or flan tin

This is a simple-to-prepare recipe which you will find as versatile as it is nutritious. Try using 2 oz/55g soya flour and ½ lb/225g wholemeal flour for a pastry which easily acquires a golden suntan and has a sweet, nutty flavour. Note, this pastry is low in fat and cholesterol-free

10 oz/285g wholemeal plain flour
A little salt to taste
2 tablespoons oil or tahini
6 oz/170g mashed tofu
A little salt to taste
Water to mix

Mix the flour and salt in a bowl and make a 'well' in the centre. Mix the oil (or tahini) into the tofu then place in the well.

Mixing from the centre using your hand, add sufficient water to bring the mixture to a scone dough consistency. Kneed lightly, then use as required.

SOYA COCONUT COOKIES

Cooking time — 15-18 minutes   Makes about 25-30

A crunchy munchie favourite

3½ oz/100g margarine
3 oz/85g raw cane sugar
1 tablespoon tahini or 1 egg, beaten
3 oz/85g desiccated coconut
4 oz/115g rice bran
2 oz/55g soya flour
2 teaspoons baking powder

Blend the margarine and sugar until creamy, then add the tahini (or egg) mixing well.

Combine the coconut, rice bran, soya flour and baking powder and stir into the blended mixture. Mix well, then form into small balls about the size of a walnut.

Place on baking sheets which have been brushed lightly with a little melted margarine or oil, allowing room for spreading between the cookies. Bake at 400°F, 200°C or Gas Mark 6 until golden brown. Allow to cool on the baking sheet then store in an airtight jar.

SOYA SESAME BREAD

Cooking time — 35-40 minutes   For 2 small loaves

2-3 teaspoons honey
½ pint/285ml hot water
8 fl oz/240ml soya milk
1 tablespoon active dried yeast or 2 tablespoons fresh
yeast
1 lb/455g wholemeal flour or 1 lb/455g unbleached
white flour
4 oz/115g soya flour
½ teaspoon sea salt
2 tablespoons toasted sesame seeds

Mix the honey, hot water and soya milk together in a bowl and sprinkle the dried yeast on top (or crumble fresh yeast into the mixture). Cover the bowl with a tea towel and leave to stand for 5 minutes to allow the yeast to become active.

Mix the wholemeal flour, soya flour, salt and toasted sesame seeds and make a well in the centre. Pour the yeast mixture into the well and mix thoroughly to form a soft dough. Knead for about 3 minutes or until the dough springs back when pressed with the flat of your finger. Cover and put in a warm place until the dough doubles in size — about 35-40 minutes

Knead again for about 1 minute. Form into 4 balls of dough and place 2 balls in each lightly oiled tin. Cover with a tea towel and place in a warm area of your kitchen until the dough doubles in size again (about 45 minutes).

Bake at 425°F, 220°C or Gas Mark 7 for about 35 minutes. The bread is cooked through if when its bottom is tapped a hollow sound is produced.

VARIATION

Add 6 oz/170g okara to the flour to give the bread an interesting texture contrast.

WHEATLESS MUNCHIES

I have devised these recipes especially for those of you who have to miss out on eating cakes and cookies containing wheat, but you will enjoy them as a special treat even if you aren't allergic to wheat.

MUESLI COOKIES

Cooking time — 18 minutes   Makes about 30

Filling and nutritious, these cookies make a scrumptious snack or lunchbox treat

3 oz/85g raw cane sugar
2 tablespoons honey
4 oz/125g margarine
I egg, beaten, or I tablespoon tahini
I level teaspoon bicarbonate of soda
4 tablespoons boiling water
6 oz/170g rolled oats
3 oz/85g desiccated coconut
2 oz/55g rice bran
4 oz/115g soya flour
3 oz/85g sultanas

Blend the sugar, honey and margarine until creamy. Add the egg (or tahini), continuing to beat well. When thoroughly combined, beat in the bicarbonate of soda which has been dissolved in boiling water.

Mix the oats, coconut, rice bran, soya flour and sultanas and add the blended mixture to it. Combine well and form the mixture into small balls — about the size of a walnut.

Allowing room for the cookies to spread a little, place on baking sheets which have been lightly brushed with a little melted margarine or oil. Bake at 400°F, 200°C or Gas Mark 6 until golden brown — about 18 minutes. Allow the cookies to cool on the sheet. When completely cold, store in an airtight container.

WONDERFUL WHEATLESS FLAN

Cooking time — 20-25 minutes   For an 8 inch/20cm flan tin

You can have your cake and eat it too

Base
6 oz/170g rolled oats
2 oz/55g soya flour
2 oz/55g rice bran
1 oz/30g ground nuts
2 tablespoons oil
1 tablespoon honey
4 fl oz/115ml soya milk

Mix the oats, flour, rice bran and nuts. Mix the oil, honey and soya milk and add to the dry ingredients. Combine well, then pat down into the base of a lightly oiled flan tin. Bake at 400°F, 200°C or Gas Mark 6 until golden brown, about 20 minutes. Cool. Meanwhile prepare topping.

Topping
¾ pint/425ml fruit juice
2 teaspoons agar agar powder
1 tablespoon honey (optional)
1 pint/570ml lightly stewed or ¾ lb/340g fresh fruit (apricots,
peaches, strawberries), sliced
Tofu cream (optional)

Heat the fruit juice and agar agar powder, stirring constantly until the juice boils. Reduce the heat and cook gently for 1 minute. Stir in the honey and cool to room temperature.

Meanwhile, arrange the stewed fruit (or fruit slices) on the flan crust. Pour agar agar mixture carefully over the fruit and allow to set. Chill in the refrigerator and for a special treat, top with Tofu cream and more fresh fruit.

FRUITY RICE AND SOYA CAKE

Cooking time — 50-60 minutes   For an 8 inch/20cm ring cake tin

Moist and delicious, this doubles as a delicious pudding

I lb 2 oz/610g cooked brown rice
4 oz/115g soya flour
4 oz/115g rice bran
I teaspoon cinnamon or mixed spice
I apple, grated
¾ lb/340g mixed fruit
2 tablespoons honey
2 tablespoons oil or tahini

Mix all the ingredients together well. Brush the ring tin with a little melted margarine or oil then line the bottom with greaseproof paper. Pour the mixture into the prepared tin, then bake at 350°F, 180°C or Gas Mark 4 until firm — about 50 minutes.

Serve hot as a pudding or allow to cool in the tin before turning out as a cake. To store, wrap the cake in a tea towel. In hot weather, keep the cake in the refrigerator.

APPLE UPSIDE-DOWN CAKE

Cooking time — 35 minutes   For an 8 inch/20cm cake tin

Sweet and spicy this is a delicious dessert treat or after-school delight

4 oz/125g margarine, melted
1 tablespoon raw cane sugar
Dusting of cinnamon
2 apples, peeled, cored and sliced
4 oz/115g soya flour
4 oz/115g rice bran
2 teaspoons baking powder
1½ oz/45g desiccated coconut
2 tablespoons honey
8 fl oz/240ml soya milk

Brush the cake tin with a little of the margarine, then line the bottom with greaseproof paper. Brush the paper with a little more of the margarine, then sprinkle the sugar over it. Dust with cinnamon, then arrange the apple slices on the cinnamon and sugar.

Sift the soya flour, rice bran and baking powder into a bowl, then mix in the coconut. Mix the remaining margarine with the honey and soya milk, then stir in the dry ingredients. Mix thoroughly, then pour on top of the apples.

Bake at 375°F, 190°C or Gas Mark 5 until golden brown and firm to the touch — about 35 minutes. Allow the cake to cool in the tin for about 20 minutes before turning out.

APPLE PIE FOR EVERYONE

Cooking time — Apples, 10 minutes   Pie, 30 minutes
For a 9½ inch/24cm flan or quiche tin

This is a scrumptious pie which is a family favourite. It's a good idea to stew the apples well before you want to use them. Chill in the refrigerator if possible. This way, the crust will retain its crispness

Crust
6 oz/170g rolled oats
2 oz/55g rice bran
2 oz/55g ground almonds
¼ teaspoon cinnamon
I tablespoon oil
I tablespoon honey
2 tablespoons hot water

Mix the oats, bran and almonds with the cinnamon. Mix the oil, honey and hot water together in a cup and add to the dry ingredients.

Combine well and, using moistened hands, press down onto the base of a lightly oiled flan or quiche tin. Bake at 400°F, 200°C or Gas Mark 6 for 20 minutes.

Filling
5 apples, peeled and cored
4 fl oz/115ml apple juice

Slice the apples and put them in a saucepan with the apple juice. Place the lid on the saucepan and cook gently until the apples become pulpy. Cool before placing on the crust to avoid the 'soggy bottom problem'.

Topping
2 tablespoons sesame seeds
2 tablespoons soya flour
2 tablespoons desiccated coconut

Mix the ingredients well and sprinkle over the apples. Bake at 400°F, 200°C or Gas Mark 6 until golden brown (about 10-12 minutes).

TOFU BLISSBALLS

Makes about 20

9 oz/250g tofu, drained well
1 tablespoon honey
2 tablespoons carob powder
1 teaspoon vanilla essence
1 tablespoon tahini
4 oz/115g ground almonds
1½ oz/45g desiccated coconut
Extra coconut for coating balls

Mix all the ingredients together thoroughly (it's best to use your hands). Form into balls about the size of a walnut, then roll in the extra coconut. Chill in the refrigerator and serve as a snack or a sweet end to a meal. Store the blissballs in the refrigerator and they will stay fresh for 4-5 days.

VARIATIONS

Try adding 1¼ oz/37g toasted sunflower seeds or chopped nuts.

Try adding 3 oz/85g sultanas or chopped dates.

'WHEATLESS' PIE CRUSTS

A tasty alternative to the usual pastry and a godsend for those allergic to wheat.
Fill these pie crusts with your favourite filling and if you require a 'top' on the
pie, simply sprinkle sesame seeds or ground nuts on top of the filling and continue
to bake until the top turns golden brown.

SESAME OAT PIE CRUST

Cooking time — 20-25 minutes   For a 9½ inch/24cm quiche or flan tin

6 oz/170g rolled oats
2oz/55g rice bran
2 oz/55g soya flour
1-2 tablespoons sesame seeds or ground almonds
2 tablespoons oil
1 tablespoon tahini
About 2 tablespoons water

Mix the oats, rice bran, soya flour and sesame seeds (or ground almonds) and
make a well in the centre. Add the oil and tahini and mix in enough water to
bring the mixture to a 'crumb crust' consistency.

Using moistened hands, press the mixture into the base and sides of a quiche
or flan tin which has been lightly brushed with a little oil.

Bake at 400°F, 200°C or Gas Mark 6 until light brown (about 20-25 minutes).
Cool and use with sweet or savoury pie fillings.

NUTTY RICE PIE CRUST

Cooking time — 20-25 minutes   For a 9½ inch/24cm quiche or flan tin

¾ lb/340g cooked brown rice
2 oz/55g rice bran or 2 oz/55g soya flour
2 oz/55g ground nuts
1 tablespoon oil
2 tablespoons tahini

Combine the brown rice, rice bran (or soya flour) and ground nuts well, then
work in the oil and tahini, mixing thoroughly. Using moistened hands, press into
the base and sides of the quiche or flan tin which has been lightly brushed with
a little oil.

Bake at 400°F, 200°C or Gas Mark 6 for 20-25 minutes, before using with your
favourite pie filling.

GOLDEN SOYA MUESLI

Cooking time — Roasting Okara, 35 minutesRoasting Muesli, 20 minutes
Makes

4 fl oz/115ml fruit juice or water
1 tablespoon honey
½ lb/225g rolled oats
3 oz/85g desiccated coconut or 4 oz/115g ground almonds
4 oz/115g rice bran
2 oz/55g nuts or seeds
1 lb 2 oz/610g roasted okara
3 oz/85g sultanas

Put the fruit juice (or water) and honey in a small saucepan and heat gently until the honey becomes runny. Cool.

Meanwhile, mix the oats, coconut (or ground almonds), bran and seeds well. Rub the honey mixture through the dry ingedients, using your hands. Spread the mixture out thinly on baking sheets and bake at 400°F, 200°C or Gas Mark 6 for 20 minutes. Cool slightly. Mix in the okara and sultanas and, when completely cool, store in an airtight container.

Use as a snack or breakfast food, especially delicious with fresh fruit in season and yoghurt or soya milk.

INDEX

VEGETARIAN SUPER SOYA FOODS

VEGETARIAN HIGH FIBRE COOKING

How to Safely Increase Dietary Fibre in Everyday Meals

Janette Marshall

Previously published as *High-fibre Cooking* in the 'Cooking for Special Diets' series, this completely revised and updated edition has incorporated eight pages of full colour and over a dozen replacement recipes.

Dietary fibre is good for you. It is beneficial for those with problems of obesity, diabetes, low-sugar, heart disease, constipation, varicose veins, high blood-pressure and hiatus hernia, amongst many other complaints.

However, increasing your fibre intake should be accomplished gradually, changing from processed and refined foods to a wholefood diet. Janette Marshall sets out clear guidelines for building natural fibre into your daily diet, with a wide range of mouth-watering recipes and a comprehensive list of menu suggestions, designed to inspire you to a healthier way of eating.

Janette Marshall was, until recently, deputy editor of Here's Health, *the leading magazine in the field of natural health. She is now a freelance author and journalist in all areas of alternative lifestyles, healthy living and consumer issues. Her previous titles include* The Wholefood Party Book *and* The Wholefood Cookery Course *with Sarah Bounds.*